GOVERNORS STATE UNIVERSITY
MAT-CTR.PS613.P44   C001
PECK, RICHARD, COMP.
SOUNDS AND SILENCES NEW YORK   MAX

3 1611 00014 7352

S0-ASH-894

134707

PS   Peck, Richard.
613   Sounds and
.P44   silences.
            134707

UNIVERSITY LIBRARY
Governors State University
Park Forest South, Il. 60466

SOUNDS AND SILENCES

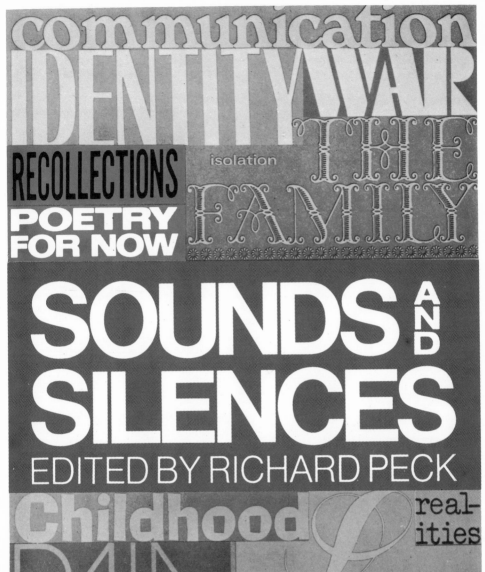

communication

IDENTITY WAR

RECOLLECTIONS

isolation

THE FAMILY

POETRY FOR NOW

SOUNDS AND SILENCES

EDITED BY RICHARD PECK

Childhood

realities

PAIN

Love

DISSENT

ILLUSION

DELACORTE PRESS / NEW YORK, N.Y.

University Library
GOVERNORS STATE UNIVERSITY

I am grateful to Mrs. Harriet Aufses, librarian of
Hunter College High School, New York City,
and to Mr. Curtis Crotty of the English Department
of Evanston Township High School, Evanston, Illinois,
for their great help and encouragement
in the compiling of this collection.

Copyright © 1970 by Richard Peck

All rights reserved. No part of this book may be
reproduced in any form or by any means without
the prior written permission of the Publisher, excepting
brief quotes used in connection with reviews written
specifically for inclusion in a magazine or newspaper.

Acknowledgments for copyrighted material
appear on pages 173 through 178
and constitute an extension of this page.

Library of Congress Catalog Card Number: 77–87167
Manufactured in the United States of America
Third Printing—1973

DESIGNED BY *Larry Kamp*

P S
6 13
.P44

TO MY MOTHER AND FATHER

TABLE OF CONTENTS

ILLUSION 77

DISSENT 91

COMMUNICATION   109

LOVE   117

WAR   129

INTRODUCTION

Once upon a time poetry knew its place: the schoolroom, the tomb-stone, and the love letter. But that was before the poetry explosion. Today, the love lyric and the protest song compete, and they compete through millions of television sets and stereo records. Poetry knows no bounds. You're liable to encounter it anywhere and on any topic. Worse yet, nobody can tell you exactly what poetry is or isn't.

When you think of "modern poetry," you may visualize words spattering a page in random pattern, mysterious fragments of meaning, or lines that refuse to rhyme. But poetry today deserves a closer analysis. We have among us men and women who write to communicate what being alive in the mid-twentieth century is like. Some of them have revolted against the traditional forms. Some of them have infused the old forms with new meaning. Some of them want their works sung in coffee houses to the strumming of guitars. Others require the utter silence of solitude. But they all want to communicate.

And what are they saying? Well, they're saying what we're all feeling. That love is seldom all hearts-and-flowers and that war is never glorious. That it's usually impossible to express your love, your anger, your self in an impersonal world. That objects man has made—aircraft and laundromats, motorcycles and moon rockets —can destroy a world he is trying to improve. That tensions in this tense age result from the conflict between public life and private life, between realities and illusions.

In short, contemporary poetry has drawn nearer to the world of its reader—life as it's lived, more than life as it should be. The topics that hit headlines often inspire poems. There will, I expect, always be poetry about love, death, and nature. But at this point in time, poetry has burst out of its old confinements and refuses to be neatly limited. This is vastly important to us all because a poem can often be truer than a headline.

Most of the poetry in this collection was written in your lifetime. Most of it was written by poets whose works you will encounter again and again with the growing awareness that poets occupy the same space and time span that their readers do. That what concerns the reader concerns the writer.

SOUNDS AND SILENCES follows a pattern familiar to every one of us. *The Family:* its members and relationships. *Childhood:* when we begin to move from the people who gave us life to lives of our own. *Isolation:* where we begin to develop ideas about our most private selves. *Identity:* the quest for achieving that self. *Realities:* the unavoidable and concrete aspects of our world. *Illusions:* the unreal that conflicts with the real. *Dissent:* that growing problem in a standardized world. *Communication:* the need for rapport. *Love:* the timeless topic which depends upon communication. *War:* the threat to every human impulse. *Pain:* war's inevitable companion. And, finally, *Recollections:* a second look at things that linger in the mind.

No poet has the final word on any of these topics. But each poet has his view. Hopefully, there will be times—many times—when you can say, "That's the way I feel too." I think that's what the poets want. That's what has led them to write poetry on "unpoetic" themes. So be prepared to find in this collection the unexpected, but familiar: sonic booms, conscientious objectors, bombers, migrant workers, psychedelic images, lifeguards, train wrecks, and revolution. Be prepared, too, to find yourself.

RICHARD PECK
New York

THE FAMILY

LITTLE BRAND NEW BABY

Hey, Little Brand New Baby,
Your Momma and your Daddy think you're mighty nice.
Hey, Little Brand New Baby,
I hope you have a mighty nice life.

Your Daddy's lookin' mighty proud,
Handin' out cigars all around the town,
grinnin' like a 'Possum
And I think he's gonna crow,
And I hope you have a mighty nice life.

Your Momma waited quite awhile,
Carried you around for half a million miles,
But you know it was worth it when you look at her smile,
And I hope you have a mighty nice life.

It all lies ahead of you and from this day
It won't be easy as you travel your way,
But here's to your birth and I just want to say
That I hope you have a mighty nice life.

TOM PAXTON

THE NAME

Be natural,
wise
as you can be,
my daughter,

let my name
be in you flesh
I gave you
in the act of

loving your mother,
all your days
her ways,
the woman in you

brought from
sensuality's measure,
no other,
there was no thought

of it but such
pleasure all women
must be in her,
as you. But not wiser,

not more of nature
than her hair,
the eyes
she gives you.

There will not be another
woman such as you
are. Remember
your mother,

the way you came,
the days of waiting.
Be natural,
daughter, wise

as you can be,
all my daughters,
be women
for men

when that time comes.
Let the rhetoric
stay with me
your father. Let

me talk about it,
saving you such
vicious self-
exposure, let you

pass it on
in you. I cannot
be more than the man
who watches.

ROBERT CREELEY

TAUGHT ME PURPLE

My mother taught me purple
Although she never wore it.
Wash-gray was her circle,
The tenement her orbit.

My mother taught me golden
And held me up to see it,
Above the broken molding,
Beyond the filthy street.

My mother reached for beauty
And for its lack she died,
Who knew so much of duty
She could not teach me pride.

EVELYN TOOLEY HUNT

MOTHER TO SON

Well, Son, I'll tell you
Life for me ain't been no crystal stair
It's had tacks in it,
And splinters,
And boards torn up,
And places with no carpets on the floor,

Bare.
But all the time
I'se been climbin' on
And reachin' landin's
And turning corners
And sometimes goin' on in the dark
Where there ain't been no light.
So, Boy, don't you turn back.
Don't you set down on the steps
'Cause you find it's kinder hard.
Don't you fall now—
For I'se still goin', Honey,
I'se still climbin'
And life for me ain't been
        no crystal stair.

LANGSTON HUGHES

THAT DARK OTHER MOUNTAIN

My father could go down a mountain faster than I
Though I was first one up.
Legs braced or with quick steps he slid
   the gravel slopes
Where I picked cautious footholds.

Black, Iron, Eagle, Doublehead, Chocorua,
Wildcat and Carter Dome—
He beat me down them all. And that last
   other mountain,
And that dark other mountain.

ROBERT FRANCIS

THE GEESE

My father was the first to hear
The passage of the geese each fall,
Passing above the house so near
He'd hear within his heart their call.

And then at breakfast time he'd say:
"The geese were heading south last night,"
For he had lain awake till day,
Feeling his earthbound soul take flight.

Knowing that winter's wind comes soon
After the rushing of those wings,
Seeing them pass before the moon,
Recalling the lure of faroff things.

RICHARD PECK

WHAT SHALL HE TELL THAT SON?

A father sees a son nearing manhood.
What shall he tell that son?
"Life is hard; be steel; be a rock."
And this might stand him for the storms
    and serve him for humdrum and monotony
    and guide him amid sudden betrayals
    and tighten him for slack moments.
"Life is soft loam; be gentle; go easy."
And this too might serve him.
Brutes have been gentled where lashes failed.
The growth of a frail flower in a path up
    has sometimes shattered and split a rock.
A tough will counts. So does desire.
So does a rich soft wanting.
Without rich wanting nothing arrives.
Tell him too much money has killed men
    and left them dead years before burial:
    and quest of lucre beyond a few easy needs
    has twisted good enough men
    sometimes into dry thwarted worms.
Tell him time as a stuff can be wasted.
Tell him to be a fool every so often
    and to have no shame over having been a fool
    yet learning something out of every folly
    hoping to repeat none of the cheap follies
    thus arriving at intimate understanding
    of a world numbering many fools.

Tell him to be alone often and get at himself
   and above all tell himself no lies about himself,
   whatever the white lies and protective fronts
   he may use amongst other people.
Tell him solitude is creative if he is strong
   and the final decisions are made in silent rooms.
Tell him to be different from other people
   if it comes natural and easy being different.
Let him have lazy days seeking his deeper motives.
Let him seek deep for where he is a born natural.
      Then he may understand Shakespeare
      and the Wright brothers, Pasteur, Pavlov,
      Michael Faraday and free imaginations
   bringing changes into a world resenting change.
         He will be lonely enough
         to have time for the work
         he knows as his own.

                    CARL SANDBURG

MY PAPA'S WALTZ

The whiskey on your breath
Could make a small boy dizzy;
But I hung on like death:
Such waltzing was not easy.

We romped until the pans
Slid from the kitchen shelf;
My mother's countenance
Could not unfrown itself.

The hand that held my wrist
Was battered on one knuckle;
At every step you missed
My right ear scraped a buckle.

You beat time on my head
With a palm caked hard by dirt,
Then waltzed me off to bed
Still clinging to your shirt.

THEODORE ROETHKE

THE EMPTY WOMAN

The empty woman took toys!
    In her sisters' homes
Were little girls and boys.

The empty woman had hats
To show. With feathers. Wore combs
In polished waves. Wooed cats

And pigeons. Shopped.
Shopped hard for nephew-toys,
Niece-toys. Made taffy. Popped

Popcorn and hated her sisters,
Featherless and waveless but able to
Mend measles, nag noses, blast blisters

And all day waste wordful girls
And war-boys, and all day
Say "Oh God!"—and tire among curls

And plump legs and proud muscle
And blackened school-bags, babushkas, torn socks,
And bouffants that bustle, and rustle.

GWENDOLYN BROOKS

STARK BOUGHS ON THE FAMILY TREE

Up in the attic on row on row,
In dusty frames, with stubborn eyes,
My thin ancestors slowly fade
Under the flat Ohio skies.

And so, I think, they always were:
Like their own portrait, years ago,
They paced the blue and windy fields,
Aged in the polished rooms below.

For name by name I find no sign
Of hero in this distant life,
But only men as calm as snow
Who took some faithful girl as wife,

Who labored while the drought, the flood
Crisscrossed the fickle summer air,
Who built great barns and propped their lives
Upon a slow heart-breaking care.

Why do I love them as I do,
Who dared no glory, won no fame?
In a harsh land that lies subdued,
They are the good boughs of my name.

If music sailed their dreams at all,
They were not heroes, and slept on;
As one by one they left the small
Accomplished, till the great was done.

MARY OLIVER

HOME BURIAL

He saw her from the bottom of the stairs
Before she saw him. She was starting down,
Looking back over her shoulder at some fear.
She took a doubtful step and then undid it
To raise herself and look again. He spoke
Advancing toward her: "What is it you see
From up there always—for I want to know."
She turned and sank upon her skirts at that,
And her face changed from terrified to dull.
He said to gain time: "What is it you see,"
Mounting until she cowered under him.
"I will find out now—you must tell me, dear."
She, in her place, refused him any help
With the least stiffening of her neck and silence.
She let him look, sure that he wouldn't see.
Blind creature; and a while he didn't see.
But at last he murmured, "Oh," and again, "Oh."

"What is it—what?" she said.

                 ` "Just that I see."

"You don't," she challenged. "Tell me what it is."

"The wonder is I didn't see at once.
I never noticed it from here before.
I must be wonted to it—that's the reason.
The little graveyard where my people are!
So small the window frames the whole of it.

Not so much larger than a bedroom, is it?
There are three stones of slate and one of marble,
Broad-shouldered little slabs there in the sunlight
On the sidehill. We haven't to mind *those*.
But I understand: it is not the stones,
But the child's mound—"

       "Don't, don't, don't, don't," she cried.

She withdrew shrinking from beneath his arm
That rested on the banister, and slid downstairs;
And turned on him with a daunting look,
He said twice over before he knew himself:
"Can't a man speak of his own child he's lost?"

"Not you! Oh, where's my hat? Oh, I don't need it!
I must get out of here. I must get air.
I don't know rightly whether any man can."

"Amy! Don't go to someone else this time.
Listen to me. I won't come down the stairs."
He sat and fixed his chin between his fists.
"There's something I should like to ask you, dear."

"You don't know how to ask it."

                "Help me, then."

Her fingers moved the latch for all reply.

"My words are nearly always an offense.
I don't know how to speak of anything
So as to please you. But I might be taught
I should suppose. I can't say I see how.
A man must partly give up being a man
With women-folk. We could have some arrangement
By which I'd bind myself to keep hands off
Anything special you're a-mind to name.
Though I don't like such things 'twixt those that love.
Two that don't love can't live together without them.
But two that do can't live together with them."
She moved the latch a little. "Don't—don't go.
Don't carry it to someone else this time.
Tell me about it if it's something human.
Let me into your grief. I'm not so much
Unlike other folks as your standing there
Apart would make me out. Give me my chance.
I do think, though, you overdo it a little.
What was it brought you up to think it the thing
To take your mother-loss of a first child
So inconsolably—in the face of love.
You'd think his memory might be satisfied—"

"There you go sneering now!"

                              "I'm not, I'm not!
You make me angry. I'll come down to you.
God, what a woman! And it's come to this,
A man can't speak of his own child that's dead."

"You can't because you don't know how to speak.

If you had any feelings, you that dug
With your own hand—how could you?—his little grave;
I saw you from that very window there,
Making the gravel leap and leap in air,
Leap up, like that, like that, and land so lightly
And roll back down the mound beside the hole.
I thought, Who is that man? I didn't know you.
And I crept down the stairs and up the stairs
To look again, and still your spade kept lifting.
Then you came in. I heard your rumbling voice
Out in the kitchen, and I don't know why,
But I went near to see with my own eyes.
You could sit there with the stains on your shoes
Of the fresh earth from your own baby's grave
And talk about your everyday concerns.
You had stood the spade up against the wall
Outside there in the entry, for I saw it."

"I shall laugh the worst laugh I ever laughed.
I'm cursed. God, if I don't believe I'm cursed."

"I can repeat the very words you were saying.
'Three foggy mornings and one rainy day
Will rot the best birch fence a man can build.'
Think of it, talk like that at such a time!
What had how long it takes a birch to rot
To do with what was in the darkened parlor.

You *couldn't* care! The nearest friends can go
With anyone to death, comes so far short
They might as well not try to go at all.
No, from the time when one is sick to death,
One is alone, and he dies more alone.

Friends make pretense of following to the grave,
But before one is in it, their minds are turned
And making the best of their way back to life
And living people, and things they understand.
But the world's evil. I won't have grief so
If I can change it. Oh, I won't, I won't!"

"There, you have said it all and you feel better.
You won't go now. You're crying. Close the door.
The heart's gone out of it: why keep it up.
Amy! There's someone coming down the road!"

"*You*—oh, you think the talk is all. I must go—
Somewhere out of this house. How can I make you—"

"If—you—do!" She was opening the door wider.
"Where do you mean to go? First tell me that.
I'll follow and bring you back by force. I *will!*—"

ROBERT FROST

Childhood

DECLARATION OF INDEPENDENCE *

He will just do nothing at all.
He will just sit there in the noon-day sun.
And when they speak to him;—
he will not answer them
because he does not wish to
And when they tell him to eat his dinner
he will just laugh at them,
And he will not take his nap
Because he does not care to.
He will just sit there in the noon-day sun.
He will go away—and play with the panda,
and when they come to look for him,
he will stick them with spears
And put them in the garbage and put the cover on
And he will not go out in the fresh air.
nor eat his vegetables
And he will grow thin as a marble
He will just do nothing at all.
He will just sit there in the noon-day sun.

WOLCOTT GIBBS

* Wolcott Gibbs heard this sung one evening by his
four-year-old son in the bathtub, and got the words
printed in *The New Yorker*. Celius Dougherty later
set it to music.

DRAWING BY RONNIE C., GRADE ONE

For the sky, blue. But the six-year-
old searching his crayon-box, finds
no blue to match that sky
framed by the window—a see-through
   shine
over treetops, housetops. The wax colors
hold only dead light, not this water-
   flash
thinning to silver
at morning's far edge.
Gray won't do, either:
gray is for rain that you make with
dark slanting lines down-paper

                              Try orange!

—Draw a large corner circle for sun,
  egg-yolk solid,
with yellow strokes, leaping outward
like fire bloom—a brightness shouting
flower-shape   wind-shape   joy-shape!

The boy sighs, with leg-twisting bliss
  creating . . .

It is done. The stubby crayons
 (all ten of them) are stuffed back
bumpily into their box.

                    RUTH LECHLITNER

MY PARENTS KEPT ME FROM
CHILDREN WHO WERE ROUGH

My parents kept me from children who were rough
Who threw words like stones and who wore torn clothes.
Their thighs showed through rags. They ran in the street
And climbed cliffs and stripped by the country streams.

I feared more than tigers their muscles like iron
Their jerking hands and their knees tight on my arms.
I feared the salt-coarse pointing of those boys
Who copied my lisp behind me on the road.

They were lithe, they sprang out behind hedges
Like dogs to bark at my world. They threw mud
While I looked the other way, pretending to smile.
I longed to forgive them, but they never smiled.

STEPHEN SPENDER

BOY AT THE WINDOW

Seeing the snowman standing all alone
In dusk and cold is more than he can bear.
The small boy weeps to hear the wind prepare
A night of gnashings and enormous moan.
His tearful sight can hardly reach to where
The pale-faced figure with bitumen eyes
Returns him such a god-forsaken stare
As outcast Adam gave to Paradise.

The man of snow is, nonetheless, content,
Having no wish to go inside and die.
Still, he is moved to see the youngster cry.
Though frozen water is his element,
He melts enough to drop from one soft eye
A trickle of the purest rain, a tear
For the child at the bright pane surrounded by
Such warmth, such light, such love,
   and so much fear.

RICHARD WILBUR

THE BALLAD OF THE
LIGHT-EYED LITTLE GIRL

Sweet Sally took a cardboard box,
And in went pigeon poor.
Whom she had starved to death but not
For lack of love, be sure.

The wind it harped as twenty men.
The wind it harped like hate.
It whipped our light-eyed little girl,
It made her wince and wait.

It screeched a hundred elegies
As it punished her light eyes
(Though only kindness covered these)
And it made her eyebrows rise.

"Now bury your bird," the wind it bawled,
"And bury him down and down
Who had to put his trust in one
So light-eyed and so brown.

"So light-eyed and so villainous,
Who whooped and who could hum
But could not find the time to toss
Confederate his crumb."

She has taken her passive pigeon poor
She has buried him down and down.
He never shall sally to Sally
Nor soil any roofs of the town.

She has sprinkled nail polish on dead dandelions.
And children have gathered around
Funeral for him whose epitaph
Is "Pigeon—Under the Ground."

GWENDOLYN BROOKS

THE BALLAD OF CHOCOLATE MABBIE

It was Mabbie without the grammar school gates.
And Mabbie was all of seven.
And Mabbie was cut from a chocolate bar.
And Mabbie thought life was heaven.

The grammar school gates were the pearly gates,
For Willie Boone went to school.
When she sat by him in history class
Was only her eyes were cool.

It was Mabbie without the grammar school gates
Waiting for Willie Boone.
Half hour after the closing bell!
He would surely be coming soon.

Oh, warm is the waiting for joys, my dears!
And it cannot be too long.
Oh, pity the little poor chocolate lips
That carry the bubble of song!

Out came the saucily bold Willie Boone.
It was woe for our Mabbie now.
He wore like a jewel a lemon-hued lynx
With sand-waves loving her brow.

It was Mabbie alone by the grammar school gates.
Yet chocolate companions had she:
Mabbie on Mabbie with hush in the heart.
Mabbie on Mabbie to be.

GWENDOLYN BROOKS

JANET WAKING

Beautifully Janet slept
Till it was deeply morning. She woke then
And thought about her dainty-feathered hen,
To see how it had kept.

One kiss she gave her mother.
Only a small one gave she to her daddy
Who would have kissed each curl of his shining baby;
No kiss at all for her brother.

"Old Chucky, old Chucky!" she cried,
Running across the world upon the grass
To Chucky's house, and listening. But alas,
Her Chucky had died.

It was a transmogrifying bee
Came droning down on Chucky's old bald head
And sat and put the poison. It scarcely bled,
But how exceedingly

And purply did the knot
Swell with the venom and communicate
Its rigor! Now the poor comb stood up straight
But Chucky did not.

So there was Janet
Kneeling on the wet grass, crying her brown hen
(Translated far beyond the daughters of men)
To rise and walk upon it.

And weeping fast as she had breath
Janet implored us, "Wake her from her sleep!"
And would not be instructed in how deep
Was the forgetful kingdom of death.

                    JOHN CROWE RANSOM

PRAYER BEFORE BIRTH

I am not yet born; O hear me.
  Let not the bloodsucking bat or the rat or the stoat or the
  club-footed ghoul come near me.

I am not yet born, console me.
I fear that the human race may with tall walls wall me,
  with strong drugs dope me, with wise lies lure me,
  on black racks rack me, in blood-baths roll me.

I am not yet born; provide me
With water to dandle me, grass to grow for me, trees to talk
  to me, sky to sing to me, birds and a white light
    in the back of my mind to guide me.

I am not yet born; forgive me
For the sins that in me the world shall commit, my words
  when they speak me, my thoughts when they think me,
    my treason engendered by traitors beyond me,
      my life when they murder by means of my
        hands, my death when they live me.

I am not yet born; rehearse me
In the parts I must play and the cues I must take when
  old men lecture me, bureaucrats hector me, mountains
    frown at me, lovers laugh at me, the white
      waves call me to folly and the desert calls
        me to doom and the beggar refuses
          my gift and my children curse me.

I am not yet born; O hear me,
Let not the man who is beast or who thinks he is God
   come near me.

I am not yet born; O fill me
With strength against those who would freeze my
   humanity, would dragoon me into a lethal automaton,
      would make me a cog in a machine, a thing with
         one face, a thing, and against all those
           who would dissipate my entirety, would
             blow me like thistledown hither and
               thither or hither and thither
                 like water held in the
                   hands would spill me.

Let them not make me a stone and let them not spill me.
Otherwise kill me.

LOUIS MAC NEICE

isolation

PORTRAIT OF A GIRL
WITH COMIC BOOK

Thirteen's no age at all. Thirteen is nothing.
It is not wit, or powder on the face,
Or Wednesday matinees, or misses' clothing,
Or intellect, or grace.
Twelve has its tribal customs. But thirteen
is neither boys in battered cars nor dolls,
Not *Sara Crewe* or movie magazine,
Or pennants on the walls.

Thirteen keeps diaries and tropical fish
(A month, at most) ; scorns jumpropes in the spring;
Could not, would fortune grant it, name its wish;
Wants nothing, everything;
Has secrets from itself, friends it despises;
Admits none of the terrors that it feels;
Owns a half a hundred masks but no disguises;
And walks upon its heels.

Thirteen's anomalous—not that, not this:
Not folded bud, or wave that laps a shore,
Or moth proverbial from the chrysalis.
Is the one age defeats the metaphor.
Is not a town, like childhood, strongly walled
But easily surrounded; is no city.
Nor, quitted once, can it be quite recalled—
Not even with pity.

PHYLLIS MC GINLEY

FIFTEEN

South of the bridge on Seventeenth
I found back of the willows one summer
day a motorcycle with engine running
as it lay on its side, ticking over
slowly in the high grass. I was fifteen.

I admired all that pulsing gleam, the
shiny flanks, the demure headlights
fringed where it lay; I led it gently
to the road and stood with that
companion, ready and friendly. I was fifteen.

We could find the end of a road, meet
the sky on out Seventeenth. I thought about
hills, and patting the handle got back a
confident opinion. On the bridge we indulged
a forward feeling, a tremble. I was fifteen.

Thinking, back farther in the grass I found
the owner, just coming to, where he had flipped
over the rail. He had blood on his hand, was pale—
I helped him walk to his machine. He ran his hand
over it, called me good man, roared away.

I stood there, fifteen.

WILLIAM STAFFORD

THE DREAMER

He spent his childhood hours in a den
of rushes, watching the gray rain braille
the surface of the river. Concealed
from the outside world, nestled within,
he was safe from parents, God, and eyes
that looked upon him accusingly,
as though to say: Even at your age,
you could do better. His camouflage
was scant, but it served, and at evening,
when fireflies burned holes into heaven,
he took the path homeward in the dark,
a small Noah, leaving his safe Ark.

WILLIAM CHILDRESS

THE CAVE

Sometimes when the boy was troubled he would go
   To a little cave of stone above the brook
And build a fire just big enough to glow
   Upon the ledge outside, then sit and look.
Below him was the winding silver trail
   Of water from the upland pasture springs,
And meadows where he heard the calling quail;
   Before him was the sky, and passing wings.

The tang of willow twigs he lighted there,
   Fragrance of meadows breathing slow and deep,
The cave's own musky coolness on the air,
   The scent of sunlight . . . all were his to keep.
We had such places—cave or tree or hill . . .
   And we are lucky if we keep them still.

GLENN W. DRESBACH

PREFACE TO A TWENTY VOLUME
SUICIDE NOTE

Lately, I've become accustomed to the way
The ground opens up and envelops me
Each time I go out to walk the dog.
Or the broad edged silly music the wind
Makes when I run for a bus—

Things have come to that.

And now, each night I count the stars,
And each night I get the same number.
And when they will not come to be counted
I count the holes they leave.

Nobody sings anymore.

And then last night, I tiptoed up
To my daughter's room and heard her
Talking to someone, and when I opened
The door, there was no one there . . .
Only she on her knees,
Peeking into her own clasped hands.

LEROI JONES

PASTORAL

When I was younger
it was plain to me
I must make something of myself.
Older now
I walk back streets
admiring the houses
of the very poor:
roof out of line with sides
the yards cluttered
with old chicken wire, ashes,
furniture gone wrong;
the fences and outhouses
built of barrel-staves
and parts of boxes, all,
if I am fortunate,
smeared a bluish green
that properly weathered
pleases me best
of all colors.

No one
will believe this
of vast import to the nation.

WILLIAM CARLOS WILLIAMS

IDENTITY

KENNEDY

I think that what he gave us most was pride.
It felt good to have a President like that:
bright, brave and funny and goodlooking.

I saw him once drive down East Seventy-second Street
in an open car, in the autumn sun
(as he drove yesterday in Dallas) .
His thatch of brown hair looked as though it had grown extra thick
the way our wood animals in Connecticut
grow extra fur for winter.
And he looked as though it was fun to be alive,
to be a politician,
to be President,
to be a Kennedy,
to be a man.

MOLLY KAZAN

YET DO I MARVEL

I doubt not God is good, well-meaning, kind,
And did He stoop to quibble could tell why
The little buried mole continues blind,
Why flesh that mirrors Him must some day die,
Make plain the reason tortured Tantalus
Is baited by the fickle fruit, declare
If merely brute caprice dooms Sisyphus
To struggle up a never-ending stair.
Inscrutable His ways are, and immune
To catechism by a mind too strewn
With petty cares to slightly understand
What awful brain compels His awful hand.
Yet do I marvel at this curious thing:
To make a poet black, and bid him sing!

COUNTEE CULLEN

THE NEGRO SPEAKS OF RIVERS

I've known rivers:
I've known rivers ancient as the world and older than the flow of
    human blood in human veins.

My soul has grown deep like the rivers.

I bathed in the Euphrates when dawns were young.
I built my hut near the Congo and it lulled me to sleep.
I looked upon the Nile and raised the pyramids above it.
I heard the singing of the Mississippi when Abe Lincoln went
    down to New Orleans, and I've seen its muddy bosom turn all
    golden in the sunset.

LANGSTON HUGHES

POWWOW *

They all see the same movies.
    They shuffle on one leg,
        Scuffing the dust up,
    Shuffle on the other.
They are all the same:
    A Sioux dance to the spirits,
    A war dance by four Chippewa,
    A Dakota dance for rain.
        We wonder why we came.
Even tricked out in the various braveries—
    Black buffalo tassels, beadwork, or the brilliant
    Feathers at the head, at the buttocks—
Even in long braids and the gaudy face paints,
        They all dance with their eyes turned
    Inward, like a woman nursing
A sick child she already knows
    Will die. For the time, she nurses it
    All the same. The loudspeakers shriek;
        We leave our bleacher seats to wander
    Among the wickiups and lean-tos
In a search for hot dogs. The Indians
        Are already packing; have
    Resumed green dungarees and khaki,
    Castoff combat issues of World War II.
        (Only the Iroquois do not come here;
They work in structural steel; they have a contract
    Building the United Nations

* Tama Reservation, Iowa, 1949.

And Air Force installations for our future wars.)
These, though, have dismantled their hot-dog stand
        And have to drive all night
To jobs in truck stops and all-night filling stations.
        We ask directions and
    They scuttle away from us like moths.
        Past the trailers,
    Beyond us, one tepee is still shining
Over all the rest. Inside, circled by a ring
        Of children, in the glare
    Of one bare bulb, a shrunken fierce-eyed man
Squats at his drum, all bones and parchment,
        While his dry hands move
    On the drumhead, always drumming, always
Raising his toothless, drawn jaw to the light
    Like a young bird drinking, like a chained dog,
Howling his tribe's song for the restless young
        Who wander in and out.
        Words of such great age,
Not even he remembers what they mean.
        We tramp back to our car,
    Then nearly miss the highway, squinting
Through red and yellow splatterings on the windshield,
    The garish and beautiful remains
        Of grasshoppers and dragonflies
That go with us, that do not live again.

                                W. D. SNODGRASS

FLORIDA ROAD WORKERS

I'm makin' a road
For the cars to fly by on,
Makin' a road
Through the palmetto thicket
For light and civilization
To travel on.

I'm makin' a road
For the rich to sweep over
In their big cars
And leave me standin' here.

Sure,
A road helps everybody!
Rich folks ride—
And I get to see 'em ride.

I ain't never seen nobody
Ride so fine before.
Hey, Buddy, Look!
I'm makin' a road!

LANGSTON HUGHES

PASTURES OF PLENTY

It's a mighty hard row that my poor hands has hoed,
My poor feet has traveled a hot dusty road;
Out of your Dust Bowl and westward we rolled,
And your deserts was hot and your mountains was cold.

I worked in your orchard of peaches and prunes,
Slept on the ground 'neath the light of the moon;
On the edge of your city you will see us and then,
We come with the dust and we go with the wind.

California, Arizona, I make all your crops,
Well, it's up north to Oregon to gather your hops;
Dig the beets from your ground, cut the grapes from your vine,
To set on your table your light, sparkling wine.

Green pastures of plenty from dry desert ground,
From the Grand Coulee Dam where the waters run down;
Every state in the union us migrants has been,
We'll work in this fight and we'll fight till we win.

It's always we rambled, that river and I,
All along your green valley I will work till I die;
My land I'll defend with my life if it be,
'Cause my pastures of plenty must always be free.

WOODY GUTHRIE

CALIBAN IN THE COAL MINES

God, we don't like to complain.
　　We know that the mine is no lark.
But—there's the pools from the rain;
　　But—there's the cold and the dark.

God, You don't know what it is—
　　You, in Your well-lighted sky—
Watching the meteors whizz;
　　Warm, with a sun always by.

God, if You had but the moon
　　Stuck in Your cap for a lamp,
Even You'd tire of it soon,
　　Down in the dark and the damp.

Nothing but blackness above
　　And nothing that moves but the cars . . .
God, if You wish for our love,
　　Fling us a handful of stars!

LOUIS UNTERMEYER

SUNDAY AFTERNOON

After the First Communion
and the banquet of mangoes and
bridal cake, the young daughters
of the coffee merchant lay down
for a long siesta, and their white dresses
lay beside them in quietness
and the white veils floated
in their dreams as the flies buzzed.
But as the afternoon
burned to a close they rose
and ran about the neighborhood
among the halfbuilt villas
alive, alive, kicking a basketball, wearing
other new dresses, of bloodred velvet.

DENISE LEVERTOV

TWO VOICES IN A MEADOW

A Milkweed

Anonymous as cherubs
Over the crib of God,
White seeds are floating
Out of my burst pod.
What power had I
Before I learned to yield?
Shatter me, great wind:
I shall possess the field.

A Stone

As casual as cow-dung
Under the crib of God,
I lie where chance would have me,
Up to the ears in sod.
Why should I move? To move
Befits a light desire.
The sill of Heaven would founder,
Did such as I aspire.

RICHARD WILBUR

GONE AWAY

When my body leaves me
I'm lonesome for it.
I've got

eyes, ears,
nose and mouth
and that's all.

Eyes
keep on seeing the
feather blue of the

cold sky,
mouth takes in
hot soup,
nose

smells the frost,

ears hear everything, all
the noises and absences,
but body

goes away to I don't know where
and it's lonesome to drift
above the space it
fills when it's here.

DENISE LEVERTOV

THE REBEL

When I
die
I'm sure
I will have a
Big Funeral . . .
Curiosity
seekers . . .
coming to see
if I
am really
Dead . . .
or just
trying to make
Trouble. . . .

MARI E. EVANS

real-
ities

BENDIX

This porthole overlooks a sea
Forever falling from the sky,
The water inextricably
Involved with buttons, suds, and dye.

Like bits of shrapnel, shards of foam
Fly heavenward; a bedsheet heaves,
A stocking wrestles with a comb,
And cotton angels wave their sleeves.

The boiling purgatorial tide
Revolves our dreary shorts and slips,
While Mother coolly bakes beside
Her little jugged apocalypse.

JOHN UPDIKE

AT BREAKFAST

Not quite
spherical
White
Oddly closed
and without a lid

A smooth miracle
here in my hand
Has it slid
from my sleeve?

The shape
of this box
keels me oval
Heels feel
its bottom
Nape knocks
its top

Seated
like a foetus
I look for
the dream-seam

What's inside?
A sun?
Off with its head
though it hasn't any .
or is all head no body

a
One

Neatly
the knife scalps it
I scoop out
the braincap
soft
sweetly shuddering

Mooncream
this could be
Spoon
laps the larger
crescent
loosens a gilded
nucleus
from warm pap
A lyrical food

Opened
a seamless miracle
Ate a sun-germ
Good

MAY SWENSON

SONIC BOOM

I'm sitting in the living room,
When, up above, the Thump of Doom
Resounds. Relax. It's sonic boom.

The ceiling shudders at the clap,
The mirrors tilt, the rafters snap,
And Baby wakens from his nap.

"Hush, babe. Some pilot we equip,
Giving the speed of sound the slip,
Has cracked the air like a penny whip."

Our world is far from frightening; I
No longer strain to read the sky
Where moving fingers (jet planes) fly.
Our world seems much too tame to die.

And if it does, with one more pop,
I shan't look up to see it drop.

JOHN UPDIKE

ice cream
i scream
ice cream

bright
chosen   blurred
lucent   rounded off
sharp   made indefinite
                                                          The side
uneven   nubbled
curving   the image   syrup-slow
but willed   the transformation   the taste
jagged   glyceride
                           eating it   the memory
silent   smirched
magical, one   shimmering
moment only   insatiable

melting   accumulating,
                                                    dribbling, about
the shape itself   the cone   to drop
the texture   cardboard
a test   the surface
an admission   sticky as plastic

the recognition   immediate and
deceiving the mind   unknown
the lettering on the rim   trivial
arguing sugar crystals,   enormous
blatant, gummy, broken

                                                      licked
the patchwork grill   moist
intensifying   still
curving   firm

outline   yet
curling its   dis-
fingers   appear-
around,   ing
and down

possessing

to draw, to take
in the hand,
to crunch
its one
point

JONATHAN PRICE

THE BAT

By day the bat is cousin to the mouse.
He likes the attic of an aging house.

His fingers make a hat about his head.
His pulse beat is so slow we think him dead.

He loops in crazy figures half the night
Among the trees that face the corner light.

But when he brushes up against a screen,
We are afraid of what our eyes have seen:

For something is amiss or out of place
When mice with wings can wear a human face.

THEODORE ROETHKE

FOR A LAMB

I saw on the slant hill a putrid lamb,
Propped with daisies. The sleep looked deep,
The face nudged in the green pillow
But the guts were out for crows to eat.
Where's the lamb? whose tender plaint
Said all for the mute breezes.
Say he's in the wind somewhere,
Say, there's a lamb in the daisies.

RICHARD EBERHART

SUMMER: WEST SIDE

When on the coral-red steps of old brownstones
Puerto Rican boys, their white shirts luminous,
gather, and their laughter
conveys menace as far as Central Park West,

When the cheesecake shops on Broadway
keep open long into the dark,
and the Chinaman down in his hole of seven steps
leaves the door of his laundry ajar,
releasing a blue smell of starch,

When the indefatigable lines of parked cars
seem embedded in the tar,
and the swish of the cars on the Drive
seems urgently loud—

Then even the lapping of wavelets
on the boards of a barge on the Hudson
is audible,
and Downtown's foggy glow
fills your windows right up to the top.

And you walk in the mornings with your cool suit
sheathing the fresh tingle of your shower,
and the gratings idly steam,
and the damp path of the street-sweeper evaporates,

And—an oddly joyful sight—
the dentists' and chiropractors' white signs low
in the windows of the great ochre buildings on Eighty-sixth Street
Seem slightly darkened
by one more night's deposit of vigil.

JOHN UPDIKE

AUTO WRECK

Its quick soft silver bell beating, beating,
And down the dark one ruby flare
Pulsing out red light like an artery,
The ambulance at top speed floating down
Past beacons and illuminated clocks
Wings in a heavy curve, dips down,
And brakes speed, entering the crowd.
The doors leap open, emptying light;
Stretchers are laid out, the mangled lifted
And stowed into the little hospital.
Then the bell, breaking the hush, tolls once,
And the ambulance with its terrible cargo
Rocking, slightly rocking, moves away,
As the doors, an afterthought, are closed.

We are deranged, walking among the cops
Who sweep glass and are large and composed.
One is still making notes under the light.
One with a bucket douches ponds of blood
Into the street and gutter.
One hangs lanterns on the wrecks that cling,
Empty husks of locusts, to iron poles.

Our throats were tight as tourniquets,
Our feet were bound with splints, but now,
Like convalescents intimate and gauche,
We speak through sickly smiles and warn
With the stubborn saw of common sense,
The grim joke and the banal resolution.
The traffic moves around with care,
But we remain, touching a wound
That opens to our richest horror.

Already old, the question Who shall die?
Becomes unspoken Who is innocent?
For death in war is done by hands;
Suicide has cause and still birth, logic;
And cancer, simple as a flower, blooms.
But this invites the occult mind,
Cancels our physics with a sneer,
And spatters all we knew of denouement
Across the expedient and wicked stones.

KARL SHAPIRO

THE YACHTS

contend in a sea which the land partly encloses
shielding them from the too heavy blows
of an ungoverned ocean which when it chooses

tortures the biggest hulls, the best man knows
to pit against its beatings, and sinks them pitilessly.
Mothlike in mists, scintillant in the minute

brilliance of cloudless days, with broad bellying sails
they glide to the wind tossing green water
from their sharp prows while over them the crew crawls

ant like, solicitously grooming them, releasing,
making fast as they turn, lean far over and having
caught the wind again, side by side, head for the mark.

In a well guarded arena of open water surrounded by
lesser and greater craft which, sycophant, lumbering
and flittering follow them, they appear youthful, rare

as the light of a happy eye, live with the grace
of all that in the mind is feckless, free and
naturally to be desired. Now the sea which holds them

is moody, lapping their glossy sides, as if feeling
for some slightest flaw but fails completely.
Today no race. Then the wind comes again. The yachts

move, jockeying for a start, the signal is set and they
are off. Now the waves strike at them but they are too
well made, they slip through, though they take in canvas.

Arms with hands grasping seek to clutch at the prows.
Bodies thrown recklessly in the way are cut aside.
It is a sea of faces about them in agony, in despair

until the horror of the race dawns staggering the mind,
the whole sea become an entanglement of watery bodies
lost to the world bearing what they cannot hold. Broken,

beaten, desolate, reaching from the dead to be taken up
they cry out, failing, failing! their cries rising
in waves still as the skillful yachts pass over.

WILLIAM CARLOS WILLIAMS

CRYSTAL MOMENT

Once or twice this side of death
Things can make one hold his breath.

From my boyhood I remember
A crystal moment of September.

A wooded island rang with sounds
Of church bells in the throats of hounds.

A buck leaped out and took the tide
With jewels flowing past each side.

With his high head like a tree
He swam within a yard of me.

I saw the golden drop of light
In his eyes turned dark with fright.

I saw the forest's holiness
On him like a fierce caress.

Fear made him lovely past belief,
My heart was trembling like a leaf.

He leaned towards the land and life
With need above him like a knife.

In his wake the hot hounds churned,
They stretched their muzzles out and yearned.

They bayed no more, but swam and throbbed,
hunger drove them till they sobbed.

Pursued, pursuers reached the shore
And vanished. I saw nothing more.

So they passed, a pageant such
As only gods could witness much,

Life and death upon one tether
And running beautiful together.

ROBERT P. TRISTRAM COFFIN

TRAVELING THROUGH THE DARK

Traveling through the dark I found a deer
dead on the edge of the Wilson River road.
It is usually best to roll them into the canyon:
that road is narrow; to swerve might make more dead.

By glow of the tail-light I stumbled back of the car
and stood by the heap, a doe, a recent killing;
she had stiffened already, almost cold.
I dragged her off; she was large in the belly.

My fingers touching her side brought me the reason—
her side was warm; her fawn lay there waiting,
alive, still, never to be born.
Beside that mountain road I hesitated.

The car aimed ahead its lowered parking lights;
under the hood purred the steady engine.
I stood in the glare of the warm exhaust turning red;
around our group I could hear the wilderness listen.

I thought hard for us all—my only swerving—,
then pushed her over the edge into the river.

WILLIAM STAFFORD

from *THE MAN WITH THE BLUE GUITAR*

I

The man bent over his guitar,
A shearsman of sorts. The day was green.

They said, "You have a blue guitar,
You do not play things as they are."

The man replied, "Things as they are
Are changed upon the blue guitar."

And they said then, "But play, you must,
A tune beyond us, yet ourselves,

A tune upon the blue guitar
Of things exactly as they are."

II

I cannot bring a world quite round,
Although I patch it as I can.

I sing a hero's head, large eye
And bearded bronze, but not a man,

Although I patch him as I can
And reach through him almost to man.

If to serenade almost to man
Is to miss, by that, things as they are,

Say that it is the serenade
Of a man that plays a blue guitar.

WALLACE STEVENS

NUMBER 20

The pennycandystore beyond the El
is where I first
                    fell in love
                              with unreality
Jellybeans glowed in the semi-gloom
of that september afternoon
A cat upon the counter moved among
                              the licorice sticks
                    and tootsie rolls
          and Oh Boy Gum

Outside the leaves were falling as they died

A wind had blown away the sun

A girl ran in
Her hair was rainy
Her breasts were breathless in the little room

Outside the leaves were falling
                    and they cried
                              Too soon! too soon!

LAWRENCE FERLINGHETTI

EGO

When I was on Night Line,
flying my hands to park
a big-bird B-29,
I used to command the dark:
four engines were mine

to jazz; I was ground-crew,
an unfledged pfc,
but when I waved planes through
that flight line in Tennessee,
my yonder was wild blue.

Warming up, I was hot
on the throttle, logging an hour
of combat, I was the pilot
who rogered the tower.
I used to take off a lot.

With a flat-hat for furlough
and tin wings to sleep on,
I fueled my high-octane ego:
I buzzed, I landed my jeep on
the ramp, I flew low.

When a cross-country hop
let down, I was the big deal
who signaled big wheels to stop.
That's how I used to feel.
I used to get all revved up.

PHILIP BOOTH

LUCY IN THE SKY WITH DIAMONDS

Picture yourself in a boat on a river,
With tangerine trees and marmalade skies
Somebody calls you, you answer quite slowly,
A girl with kaleidoscope eyes.
Cellophane flowers of yellow and green,
Towering over your head.
Look for the girl with the sun in her eyes,
And she's gone.
Lucy in the sky with diamonds.
Follow her down to a bridge by a fountain
Where rocking horse people eat marshmallow pies,
Everyone smiles as you drift past the flowers,
That grow so incredibly high.
Newspaper taxis appear on the shore,
Waiting to take you away.
Climb in the back with your head in the clouds,
And you're gone.
Lucy in the sky with diamonds.
Picture yourself on a train in a station,
With plasticine porters with looking glass ties,
Suddenly someone is there at the turnstile,
The girl with the kaleidoscope eyes.

THE BEATLES

MUSEUMS

Museums offer us, running from among the 'buses,
A centrally heated refuge, parquet floors and sarcophaguses,
Into whose tall fake porches we hurry without a sound
Like a beetle under a brick that lies, useless on the ground.
Warmed and cajoled by the silence, the cowed cipher revives,
Mirrors himself in the cases of pots, paces himself by marble lives,
Makes believe it was he that was the glory that was Rome,
Soft on his cheek the nimbus of other people's martyrdom,
And then returns to the street, his mind an arena where sprawls
Any number of consumptive Keatses and dying Gauls.

LOUIS MACNEICE

SUBURBAN MADRIGAL

Sitting here in my house,
looking through my windows
diagonally at my neighbor's house,
I see his sun-porch windows;
they are filled with blue-green,
the blue-green of my car,
which I parked in front of my house,
more or less, up the street,
where I can't directly see it.

How promiscuous is
the world of appearances!
How frail are property laws!
To him his window is filled with his
things: his lamps, his plants, his radio.
How annoyed he would be to know
that my car, legally parked,
yet violates his windows,
paints them full
(to me) of myself, my car,
my well-insured '55 Fordor Ford
a gorgeous green sunset streaking his panes.

JOHN UPDIKE

SAND HILL ROAD

The landscape here is Africa
in California, scattered stands
of flattened Eucalyptus spread
their shallow horizontal hands
and make a spotted shade for leopards
or giraffes. I look for leopards
under every tree, for lions
in the grass; the passage signs
are not the tracks of elephants
but panting yellow tractors, stamping
down the bushes, trampling on
the slender trees, like elephants.

But still, the river draws a belt
of green across the brown, the veldt
is still a perfect veldt. I know
that if at dusk I climb a tree
and if the moon is bright, I could
be watching when the cautious,
softly snorting herd of bulldozers
comes watering at night.

MORTON GROSSER

THE BIG ROCK CANDY MOUNTAINS

One evenin' as the sun went down
And the jungle fire was burnin'
Down the track came a hobo hikin'
And he said: "Boys, I'm not turnin',
I'm headed fer a land that's far away
Beside the crystal fountains,
So come with me, we'll all go see
The Big Rock Candy Mountains."

In the Big Rock Candy Mountains,
There's a land that's fair and bright,
Where the handouts grow on bushes,
And you sleep out every night.
Where the boxcars are all empty,
And the sun shines every day
On the birds and the bees and the cigarette trees,
And the lemonade springs where the bluebird sings,
In the Big Rock Candy Mountains.

In the Big Rock Candy Mountains,
All the cops have wooden legs,
The bulldogs all have rubber teeth,
And the hens lay soft-boiled eggs.
The farmers' trees are full of fruit,
And the barns are full of hay.
Oh, I'm bound to go where there ain't no snow,
Where the rain don't pour, the wind don't blow,
In the Big Rock Candy Mountains.

In the Big Rock Candy Mountains,
You never change your socks,
And the little streams of alcohol
Come tricklin' down the rocks.
There the brakemen have to tip their hats
And the railroad bulls are blind.
There's a lake of stew and of whisky too,
You can paddle all around 'em in a big canoe,
In the Big Rock Candy Mountains.

In the Big Rock Candy Mountains,
All the jails are made of tin,
And you can bust right out again
As soon as you are in.
There ain't no short-handled shovels,
No axes, saws or picks.
I'm going to stay where you sleep all day,
Where they hung the Turk that invented work,
In the Big Rock Candy Mountains.

ANONYMOUS

THE LIFEGUARD

In a stable of boats I lie still,
From all sleeping children hidden.
The leap of a fish from its shadow
Makes the whole lake instantly tremble.
With my foot on the water, I feel
The moon outside.

Take the utmost of its power.
I rise and go out through the boats.
I set my broad sole upon silver,
On the skin of the sky, on the moonlight,
Stepping outward from earth onto water
In quest of the miracle.

This village of children believed
That I could perform as I dived
For one who had sunk from my sight.
I saw his cropped haircut go under.
I leapt, and my steep body flashed
Once, in the sun.

Dark drew all the light from my eyes.
Like a man who explores his death
By the pull of his slow-moving shoulders,
I hung head down in the cold,
Wide-eyed, contained, and alone
Among the weeds,

And my fingertips turned into stone
From clutching immovable blackness.
Time after time I leapt upward
Exploding in breath, and fell back
From the change in the children's faces
At my defeat.

Beneath them, I swam to the boathouse
With only my life in my arms
To wait for the lake to shine back
At the risen moon with such power
That my steps on the light of the ripples
Might be sustained.

Beneath me is nothing but brightness
Like the ghost of a snow field in summer.
As I move toward the center of the lake,
Which is also the center of the moon,
I am thinking of how I may be
The savior of one

Who has already died in my care.
The dark trees fade from around me.
The moon's dust hovers together.
I call softly out, and the child's
Voice answers through blinding water.
Patiently, slowly,

He rises, dilating to break
The surface of stone with his forehead.
He is one I do not remember
Having ever seen in his life.
The ground that I stand on is trembling
Upon his smile.

I wash the black mud from my hands.
On a light given off by the grave,
I kneel in the quick of the moon
At the heart of a distant forest
And hold in my arms a child
Of water, water, water.

JAMES DICKEY

DISSENT

SKETCH FROM LOSS OF MEMORY

On Sundays I ran my mare past
the church, leaned to her camber
at Georgetown Corner throwing
sparks from the cobbled curve.
"Never run your horse on macadam,
or shoot the minister in the heart
of his sermon with a hoofbeat,"
they told me.

           The neighbor's boy
shines his motorcycles in the evenings.
"A bum in boots," they call him.
I say: "Better boots than burned ankles."
The wet days, I spent soaping
my tack until the unguent oozed
from the pores of leather,
and two weeks braiding a quirt
from four strands of rawhide.

           The boy leans
at a windy corner, horsepower roaring
between his legs with a smell of burnt
    grease
as sweet as horse sweat. I like him,
on Sunday rousing us with his revved
    engine
from our dreams of potato pudding;
his mettle pulls my memory up
big as the noon over the barn roof.

                  SONYA DORMAN

SHE'S LEAVING HOME

Wednesday morning at five o'clock as
the day begins
Silently closing her bedroom door
Leaving the note that she hoped would
say more
She goes downstairs to the kitchen
clutching her handkerchief
Quietly turning the backdoor key
Stepping outside she is free.
She (We gave her most of our lives)
is leaving (Sacrificed most of our lives)
home (We gave her everything
        money could buy)
She's leaving home after living alone
For so many years, Bye, Bye
Father snores as his wife gets into her
dressing gown
Picks up the letter that's lying there
Standing alone at the top of the stairs
She breaks down and cries to her husband
Daddy our baby's gone.

Why would she treat us so thoughtlessly
How could she do this to me.
She (We never thought of ourselves)
is leaving (Never a thought for ourselves)
home (We struggled hard all
              our lives to get by)
She's leaving home after living alone
For so many years. Bye, Bye
Friday morning at nine o'clock she is far
away
Waiting to keep the appointment she
made
Meeting a man from the motor trade.
She (What did we do that was wrong)
is having (We didn't know it was wrong)
fun (Fun is the one thing that
              money can't buy)
Something inside that was always denied
For so many years. Bye, Bye
She's leaving home bye bye.

THE BEATLES

SOUTHBOUND ON THE FREEWAY

A tourist came in from Orbitville,
parked in the air, and said:

The creatures of this star
are made of metal and glass.

Through the transparent parts
you can see their guts.

Their feet are round and roll
on diagrams—or long

measuring tapes—dark
with white lines.

They have four eyes.
The two in the back are red.

Sometimes you can see a 5-eyed
one, with a red eye turning

on the top of his head.
He must be special—

the others respect him,
and go slow,

when he passes, winding
among them from behind.

They all hiss as they glide,
like inches, down the marked

tapes. Those soft shapes,
shadowy inside

the hard bodies—are they
their guts or their brains?

MAY SWENSON

LITTLE BOXES

Little boxes on the hillside,
Little boxes made of ticky tacky little boxes little boxes,
Little boxes all the same.
There's a green one and a pink one and a blue one and a yellow
    one,
And they're all made out of ticky tacky
and they all look just the same.

And the people in the houses all went to the University
Where they were put in boxes, little boxes, all the same.
And there's doctors and there's lawyers and there's business ex-
    ecutives
And they're all made out of ticky tacky
    and they all look just the same.

And they all play on the golf course
    and drink their martini dry

And they all have pretty children and
   the children go to school
And the children go to summer camp
   and then to the University
Where they all get put in boxes and
   they all come out the same.

And the boys go into business and
   marry and raise a family
In boxes, little boxes, little boxes
   all the same.
There's a green one and a pink one and
   a blue one and a yellow one
And they're all made out of ticky tacky
   and they all look just the same.

MALVINA REYNOLDS

TARGET

The moon holds nothing in her arms;
  She is as empty as a drum.
She is a cipher, though she charms;
  She is delectable but dumb.
She has no factories or farms,
Or men to sound the fire-alarms
  When the marauding missiles come.

We have no cause to spare that face
  Suspended fatly in the sky.
She does not help the human race.
  Surely, she shines when bats flit by
And burglars seek their burgling-place
And lovers in a soft embrace
  Among the whispering bushes lie—

But that is all. Dogs still will bark
  When cottage doors are lightly knocked,
And poachers crawl about the park
  Cursing the glint on guns halfcocked;
None of the creatures of the dark
Will, in their self-absorption, mark
  That visage growing slightly pocked.

R . P . LISTER

"next to of course god america i

"next to of course god america i
love you land of the pilgrims' and so forth oh
say can you see by the dawn's early my
country 'tis of centuries come and go
and are no more what of it we should worry
in every language even deafanddumb
thy sons acclaim your glorious name by gorry
by jingo by gee by gosh by gum
why talk of beauty what could be more beautiful than these heroic happy dead
who rushed like lions to the roaring slaughter
they did not stop to think they died instead
then shall the voice of liberty be mute?"

He spoke. And drank rapidly a glass of water

e. e. cummings

VAPOR TRAIL REFLECTED IN
THE FROG POND

1

The old watch: their
thick eyes
puff and foreclose by the moon. The young, heads
trailed by the beginnings of necks,
shiver,
in the guarantee they shall be bodies.

In the frog pond
the vapor trail of a SAC bomber creeps,

I hear its drone, drifting, high up
in immaculate ozone.

2

And I hear,
coming over the hills, America singing,
her varied carols I hear:
crack of deputies' rifles practicing their aim on stray dogs
    at night,
sput of cattleprod,
TV groaning at the smells of the human body,
curses of the soldier as he poisons, burns, grinds, and stabs
the rice of the world,
with open mouth, crying strong, hysterical curses.

3

And by rice paddies in Asia
bones
wearing a few shadows
walk down a dirt road, smashed
bloodsuckers on their heel, knowing
the flesh a man throws down in the sunshine
dogs shall eat
and the flesh that is upthrown in the air
shall be seized by birds,
shoulder blades smooth, unmarked by old feather-holes,
hands rivered
by blue, erratic wanderings of the blood,
eyes crinkled up
as they gaze up at the drifting sun that gives us our lives,
seed dazzled over the footbattered blaze of the earth.

GALWAY KINNELL

THE BODY POLITIC

I shot my friend to save my country's life,
And when the happy bullet struck him dead,
I was saluted by the drum and fife
Corps of a high school, while the traitor bled.

I never thought until I pulled the trigger
But that I did the difficult and the good.
I thought republics stood for something bigger,
For the mind of man, as Plato said they stood.

So when I heard the duty they assigned,
Shooting my friend seemed only sanity;
To keep disorder from the state of mind
Was mental rectitude, it seemed to me.

The audience dispersed. I felt depressed.
I went to where my orders issued from,
But the right number on the street was just
A vacant lot. Oh, boy, had I been dumb!

I tried to find the true address, but where?
Nobody told me what I had to know,
And secretaries sent me here and there
To other secretaries, just for show.

Poor Fred. His presence will be greatly missed
By children, and by cronies by the score.
The State (I learned too late) does not exist;
Man lives by love, and not by metaphor.

DONALD HALL

pity this busy monster,manunkind

pity this busy monster,manunkind,

not. Progress is a comfortable disease:
your victim (death and life safely beyond)

plays with the bigness of his littleness
—electrons deify one razorblade
into a mountainrange;lenses extend

unwish through curving wherewhen till unwish
returns on its unself.

                    A world of made
is not a world of born—pity poor flesh

and trees,poor stars and stones,but never this
fine specimen of hypermagical

ultraomnipotence.   We doctors know

a hopeless case if—listen:there's a hell
of a good universe next door;let's go

e. e. cummings

THE UNKNOWN CITIZEN

(To JS/07/M/378 This Marble Monument
Is Erected by the State)

He was found by the Bureau of Statistics to be
One against whom there was no official complaint,
And all the reports on his conduct agree
That, in the modern sense of an old-fashioned word, he was a
                                                        saint.
For in everything he did he served the Greater Community.
Except for the War till the day he retired
He worked in a factory and never got fired,
But satisfied his employers, Fudge Motors Inc.
Yet he wasn't a scab or odd in his views,
For his Union reports that he paid his dues,
(Our report on his Union shows it was sound)
And our Social Psychology workers found
That he was popular with his mates and liked a drink.
The Press are convinced that he bought a paper every day
And that his reactions to advertisements were normal in every
                                                        way.
Policies taken out in his name prove that he was fully insured,
And his Health-card shows he was once in hospital but left it
                                                        cured.

Both Producers Research and High-Grade Living declare
He was fully sensible to the advantages of the Installment Plan
And had everything necessary to the Modern Man,
A phonograph, a radio, a car and a frigidaire.
Our researchers into Public Opinion are content
That he held the proper opinion for the time of year;
When there was peace, he was for peace; when there was war, he
went.
He was married and added five children to the population,
Which our Eugenist says was the right number for a parent of
his generation,
And our teachers report that he never interfered with their edu-
cation.
Was he free? Was he happy? The question is absurd:
Had anything been wrong, we should certainly have heard.

W. H. AUDEN

THE ANGRY MAN

The other day I chanced to meet
An angry man upon the street—
A man of wrath, a man of war,
A man who truculently bore
Over his shoulder, like a lance,
A banner labeled "Tolerance."

And when I asked him why he strode
Thus scowling down the human road,
Scowling, he answered, "I am he
Who champions total liberty—
Intolerance being, ma'am, a state
No tolerant man can tolerate.

"When I meet rogues," he cried, "who choose
To cherish oppositional views,
Lady, like this, and in this manner,
I lay about me with my banner
Till they cry mercy, ma'am." His blows
Rained proudly on prospective foes.

Fearful, I turned and left him there
Still muttering, as he thrashed the air,
"Let the Intolerant beware!"

PHYLLIS MCGINLEY

communication

THOUGHTS WHILE DRIVING HOME

Was I clever enough? Was I charming?
  Did I make at least one good pun?
Was I disconcerting? Disarming?
  Was I wise? Was I wan? Was I fun?

  Did I answer that girl with white shoulders
  Correctly, or should I have said
  (Engagingly), "Kierkegaard smolders,
  But Eliot's ashes are dead"?

  And did I, while being a smarty,
  Yet some wry reserve slyly keep,
  So they murmured, when I'd left the party,
  "He's deep. He's deep. He's deep"?

JOHN UPDIKE

CONFESSION OVERHEARD IN A SUBWAY

You will ask how I came to be eavesdropping, in the first place.
The answer is, I was not.
The man who confessed to these several crimes (call him John
   Doe) spoke into my right ear on a crowded subway train,
   while the man whom he addressed (call him Richard Roe)
   stood at my left.
Thus, I stood between them, and they talked, or sometimes
   shouted, quite literally straight through me.
How could I help but overhear?
Perhaps I might have moved away to some other strap. But the
   aisles were full.
Besides, I felt, for some reason, curious.

"I do not deny my guilt," said John Doe. "My own, first, and
   after that my guilty knowledge of still further guilt.
I have counterfeited often, and successfully.
I have been guilty of ignorance, and talking with conviction. Of
   intolerable wisdom, and keeping silent.

Through carelessness, or cowardice, I have shortened the lives of
    better men. And the name for that is murder.
All my life I have been a receiver of stolen goods."

"Personally, I always mind my own business," said Richard Roe.
    "Sensible people don't get into those scrapes."

I was not the only one who overheard this confession.
Several businessmen, bound for home, and housewives and me-
    chanics, were within easy earshot.
A policeman sitting in front of us did not lift his eyes, at the
    mention of murder, from his paper.
Why should I be the one to report these crimes?
You will understand why this letter to your paper is anonymous.
    I will sign it: Public-spirited Citizen, and hope that it can-
    not be traced.

KENNETH FEARING

LONELINESS

I was about to go, and said so;
And I had almost started for the door.
But he was all alone in the sugar-house,
And more lonely than he'd ever been before.
We'd talked for half an hour, almost,
About the price of sugar, and how I like my school,
And he had made me drink some syrup hot,
Telling me it was better that way than when cool.

And I agreed, and thanked him for it,
And said good-bye, and was about to go.
Want to see where I was born?
He asked me quickly. How to say no?

The sugar-house looked over miles of valley.
He pointed with a sticky finger to a patch of snow
Where he was born. The house, he said, was gone.
I can understand these people better, now I know.

BROOKS JENKINS

A RITUAL TO READ TO EACH OTHER

If you don't know the kind of person I am
and I don't know the kind of person you are
a pattern that others made may prevail in the world
and following the wrong god home we may miss our star.

For there is many a small betrayal in the mind
a shrug that lets the fragile sequence break
sending with shouts the horrible errors of childhood
storming out to play through the broken dyke.

And as elephants parade holding each elephant's tail,
but if one wanders the circus won't find the park,
I call it cruel and maybe the root of all cruelty
to know what occurs but not recognize the fact.

And so I appeal to a voice, to something shadowy,
a remote important region in all who talk:
though we could fool each other, we should consider—
lest the parade of our mutual life get lost in the dark.

For it is important that awake people be awake,
or a breaking line may discourage them back to sleep;
the signals we give—yes or no, maybe—
should be clear: the darkness around us is deep.

WILLIAM STAFFORD

HOW SHE RESOLVED TO ACT

"I shall be careful to say nothing at all
About myself or what I know of him
Or the vaguest thought I have—no matter how dim,
Tonight if it so happen that he call."

And not ten minutes later the doorbell rang
And into the hall he stepped as he always did
With a face and a bearing that quite poorly hid
His brain that burned and his heart that fairly sang
And his tongue that wanted to be rid of the truth.

As well as she could, for she was very loath
To signify how she felt, she kept very still,
But soon her heart cracked loud as a coffee mill
And her brain swung like a comet in the dark
And her tongue raced like a squirrel in the park.

MERRILL MOORE

Love

FOR ANNE

With Annie gone,
Whose eyes to compare
With the morning sun?

Not that I did compare,
But I do compare
Now that she's gone.

SONG

I almost went to bed
without remembering
the four white violets
I put in the button-hole
of your green sweater

and how I kissed you then
and you kissed me
shy as though I'd
never been your lover.

LEONARD COHEN

TO BE IN LOVE

To be in love
Is to touch things with a lighter hand.

In yourself you stretch, you are well.
You look at things
Through his eyes.
              A Cardinal is red.
              A sky is blue.
Suddenly you know he knows too.
He is not there but
You know you are tasting together
The winter, or light spring weather.

His hand to take your hand is overmuch.
Too much to bear.

You cannot look in his eyes
Because your pulse must not say
What must not be said.

When he
Shuts a door—
Is not there—
Your arms are water.

And you are free
With a ghastly freedom.

You are the beautiful half
Of a golden hurt.

You remember and covet his mouth,
To touch, to whisper on.

Oh when to declare
Is certain Death!

Oh when to apprize
Is to mesmerize,

To see fall down, the Column of Gold,
Into the commonest ash.

GWENDOLYN BROOKS

SONNET

Some for a little while do love, and some for long;
And some rare few forever and for aye;
Some for the measure of a poet's song,
And some the ribbon width of a summer's day.
Some on a golden crucifix do swear,
And some in blood do plight a fickle troth;
Some struck divinely mad may only stare,
And out of silence weave an iron oath.

So many ways love has none may appear
The bitter best, and none the sweetest worst;
Strange food the hungry have been known to bear,
And brackish water slakes an utter thirst.
It is a rare and tantalizing fruit
Our hands reach for, but nothing absolute.

COUNTEE CULLEN

PLACES, LOVED ONES

No, I have never found
The place where I could say
This is my proper ground,
Here I shall stay;
Nor met that special one
Who has an instant claim
On everything I own
Down to my name;
To find such seems to prove
You want no choice in where
To build, or whom to love;
You ask them to bear
You off irrevocably,
So that it's not your fault
Should the town turn dreary,
The girl a dolt.

Yet, having missed them, you're
Bound, none the less, to act
As if what you settled for
Mashed you, in fact;
And wiser to keep away
From thinking you still might trace
Uncalled-for to this day
Your person, your place.

PHILIP LARKIN

somewhere i have never travelled

somewhere i have travelled,gladly beyond
any experience,your eyes have their silence:
in your most frail gesture are things which enclose
    me,
or which i cannot touch because they are too near

your slightest look easily will unclose me
though i have closed myself as fingers,
you open always petal by petal myself as Spring opens
(touching skilfully,mysteriously)her first rose

or if your wish be to close me,i and
my life will shut very beautifully,suddenly,
as when the heart of this flower imagines
the snow carefully everywhere descending;

nothing which we are to perceive in this world equals
the power of your intense fragility:whose texture
compels me with the colour of its countries,
rendering death and forever with each breathing

(i do not know what it is about you that closes
and opens;only something in me understands
the voice of your eyes is deeper than all roses)
nobody,not even the rain,has such small hands

                                        e. e. cummings

FOR HETTIE

My wife is left-handed,
Which implies a fierce de-
termination. A complete other
worldliness. IT'S WIERD BABY
The way some folks
are always trying to be different.
A sin and a shame.

But then, she's been a bohemian
all her life . . . black stockings,
refusing to take orders. I sit
patiently, trying to tell her
what's right. TAKE THAT DAMM
PENCIL OUTTA THAT HAND. YOU'RE
RITING BACKWARDS and such. But,
to no avail. And it shows
in her work. Left-handed coffee,
left-handed eggs: when she comes
in at night . . . it's her left hand
offered for me to kiss. DAMM.

And now her belly droops over the seat.
They say it's a child. But
I ain't quite so sure.

LEROI JONES

THE RIVER-MERCHANT'S WIFE: A LETTER

While my hair was still cut straight across my forehead
I played about the front gate, pulling flowers.
You came by on bamboo stilts, playing horse,
You walked about my seat, playing with blue plums.
And we went on living in the village of Chokan:
Two small people, without dislike or suspicion.

At fourteen I married My Lord you.
I never laughed, being bashful.
Lowering my head, I looked at the wall.
Called to, a thousand times, I never looked back.

At fifteen I stopped scowling,
I desired my dust to be mingled with yours
Forever and forever and forever.
Why should I climb the look out?

At sixteen you departed,
You went into far Ku-to-yen, by the river of swirling eddies,
And you have been gone five months.
The monkeys make sorrowful noise overhead.

You dragged your feet when you went out.
By the gate now, the moss is grown, the different mosses,
Too deep to clear them away!
The leaves fall early this autumn, in wind.
The paired butterflies are already yellow with August
Over the grass in the West garden;
They hurt me. I grow older.
If you are coming down through the narrows of the river Kiang,
Please let me know beforehand,
And I will come out to meet you
     As far as Cho-fu-sa.

                                        R I H A K U *

* *Rihaku:* the Japanese name for Li Po, the Chinese poet
(705–762). Ezra Pound reconstructed several poems by Li Po.

WAR

THE SONNET-BALLAD *

O mother, mother, where is happiness?
They took my lover's tallness off to war.
Left me lamenting. Now I cannot guess
What I can use an empty heart-cup for.
He won't be coming back here any more.
Some day the war will end, but, oh, I knew
When he went walking grandly out that door
That my sweet love would have to be untrue.
Would have to be untrue. Would have to court
Coquettish death, whose impudent and strange
Possessive arms and beauty (of a sort)
Can make a hard man hesitate—and change.
And he will be the one to stammer, "Yes."
Oh mother, mother, where is happiness?

                                GWENDOLYN BROOKS

* Number 3 from "Appendix to the Anniad" leaves from
a loose-leaf war diary.

WHERE HAVE ALL
THE FLOWERS GONE?

Where have all the flowers gone,
Long time passing?
Where have all the flowers gone,
Long time ago?
Where have all the flowers gone?
The girls have picked them every one.
Oh, when will you ever learn?
Oh, when will you ever learn?

Where have all the young girls gone,
Long time passing?
Where have all the young girls gone,
Long time ago?
Where have all the young girls gone?
They've taken husbands every one.
Oh, when will you ever learn?
Oh, when will you ever learn?

Where have all the young men gone,
Long time passing?
Where have all the young men gone,
Long time ago?
Where have all the young men gone?
They're all in uniform.
Oh, when will we ever learn?
Oh, when will we ever learn?

Where have all the soldiers gone,
Long time passing?
Where have all the soldiers gone,
Long time ago?
Where have all the soldiers gone?
They've gone to graveyards, every one.
Oh, when will they ever learn?
Oh, when will they ever learn?

Where have all the graveyards gone,
Long time passing?
Where have all the graveyards gone,
Long time ago?
Where have all the graveyards gone?
They're covered with flowers every one.
Oh, when will they ever learn?
Oh, when will they ever learn?

Where have all the flowers gone,
Long time passing?
Where have all the flowers gone,
Long time ago?
Where have all the flowers gone?
Young girls picked them every one.
Oh, when will they ever learn?
Oh, when will they ever learn?

PETE SEEGER

NAMING OF PARTS

To-day we have naming of parts. Yesterday,
We had daily cleaning. And to-morrow morning,
We shall have what to do after firing. But to-day,
To-day we have naming of parts. Japonica
Glistens like coral in all of the neighbouring gardens,
    And to-day we have naming of parts.

This is the lower sling swivel. And this
Is the upper sling swivel, whose use you will see,
When you are given your slings. And this is the piling swivel,
Which in your case you have not got. The branches
Hold in the gardens their silent, eloquent gestures,
    Which in our case we have not got.

This is the safety-catch, which is always released
With an easy flick of the thumb. And please do not let me
See anyone using his finger. You can do it quite easy
If you have any strength in your thumb. The blossoms
Are fragile and motionless, never letting anyone see
    Any of them using their finger.

And this you can see is the bolt. The purpose of this
Is to open the breech, as you see. We can slide it
Rapidly backwards and forwards: we call this
Easing the spring. And rapidly backwards and forwards
The early bees are assaulting and fumbling the flowers:
      They call it easing the Spring.

They call it easing the Spring: it is perfectly easy
If you have any strength in your thumb: like the bolt,
And the breech, and the cocking-piece, and the point of balance,
Which in our case we have not got; and the almond-blossom
Silent in all of the gardens and the bees going backwards and
                                      forwards,
      For to-day we have naming of parts.

HENRY REED

OF BOMBS AND BOYS

Among boy-crawling bamboo
the slowburn fuse
ignites

a greenflow serpent hisses
whips
        coils
                strikes
        recoils
fangs deepsunk
in a fortune cookie

the jungle blossoms
a starspangled second

        scatter of fireworms

the ember Deep Hurt glows
in the no sound

RICHARD CORBIN

my sweet old etcetera

my sweet old etcetera
aunt lucy during the recent

war could and what
is more did tell you just
what everybody was fighting

for,
my sister

isabel created hundreds
(and
hundreds) of socks not to
mention shirts fleaproof earwarmers

etcetera wristers etcetera, my
mother hoped that

i would die etcetera
bravely of course my father used
to become hoarse talking about how it was
a privilege and if only he
could meanwhile my

self etcetera lay quietly
in the deep mud et

cetera
(dreaming,
et
        cetera, of
Your smile
eyes knees and of your Etcetera)

                              e. e. cummings

THE DEATH OF THE BALL
TURRET GUNNER

From my mother's sleep I fell into the State,
And I hunched in its belly till my wet fur froze.
Six miles from earth, loosed from its dream of life,
I woke to black flak and the nightmare fighters.
When I died they washed me out of the turret with a hose.

RANDALL JARRELL

AN IRISH AIRMAN
FORESEES HIS DEATH

I know that I shall meet my fate
Somewhere among the clouds above;
Those that I fight I do not hate,
Those that I guard I do not love;
My country is Kiltartan Cross,
My countrymen Kiltartan's poor,
No likely end could bring them loss
Or leave them happier than before.
Nor law, nor duty bade me fight,
Nor public men, nor cheering crowds,
A lonely impulse of delight
Drove to this tumult in the clouds;
I balanced all, brought all to mind,
The years to come seemed waste of breath,
A waste of breath the years behind
In balance with this life, this death.

WILLIAM BUTLER YEATS

ULTIMA RATIO REGUM

The guns spell money's ultimate reason
In letters of lead on the Spring hillside.
But the boy lying dead under the olive trees
Was too young and too silly
To have been notable to their important eye.
He was a better target for a kiss.

When he lived, tall factory hooters never summoned him.
Nor did restaurant plate-glass doors revolve to wave him in.
The world maintained its traditional wall
Round the dead with their gold sunk deep as a well,
Whilst his life, intangible as a Stock Exchange rumor,
                                        drifted outside.

O too lightly he threw down his cap
One day when the breeze threw petals from the trees.
The unflowering wall sprouted with guns,
Machine-gun anger quickly scythed the grasses.
Flags and leaves fell from hands and branches;
The tweed cap rotted in the nettles.

Consider his life which was valueless
In terms of employment, hotel ledgers, news files.
Consider. One bullet in ten thousand kills a man.
Ask. Was so much expenditure justified
On the death of one so young, and so silly
Lying under the olive trees, O world, O death?

STEPHEN SPENDER

THE CONSCIENTIOUS OBJECTOR

The gates clanged and they walked you into jail
More tense than felons but relieved to find
The hostile world shut out, the flags that dripped
From every mother's windowpane, obscene
The bloodlust sweating from the public heart,
The dog authority slavering at your throat.
A sense of quiet, of pulling down the blind
Possessed you. Punishment you felt was clean.

The decks, the catwalks, and the narrow light
Composed a ship. This was a mutinous crew
Troubling the captains for plain decencies,
A Mayflower brim with pilgrims headed out
To establish new theocracies to west,
A Noah's ark coasting the topmost seas
Ten miles above the sodomites and fish.
These inmates loved the only living doves.

Like all men hunted from the world you made
A good community, voyaging the storm
To no safe Plymouth or green Ararat;
Trouble or calm, the men with Bibles prayed,
The gaunt politicals construed our hate.
The opposite of all armies, you were best
Opposing uniformity and yourselves;
Prison and personality were your fate.

You suffered not so physically but knew
Maltreatment, hunger, ennui of the mind.
Well might the soldier kissing the hot beach
Erupting in his face damn all your kind.
Yet you who saved neither yourselves nor us
Are equally with those who shed the blood
The heroes of our cause. Your conscience is
What we come back to in the armistice.

KARL SHAPIRO

I'VE GOT TO KNOW

Why do your warships sail on my waters?
Why do your bombs drop down from my sky?
Why do you burn my towns and my cities?
I want to know, friend, I want to know why!

Chorus: I've got to know, friend, I've got to know!
Hungry lips ask me wherever I go!
Comrades and friends all falling around me,
I've got to know, friend, I've got to know.

Why do these boats haul death to my people?
Nitro explosives, cannons and guns?
Where is my food, my soap and my warm clothes?
I've got to know, friend, I've got to know. (Chorus)

You keep me in jail and you lock me in prison.
Your hospital's jammed, and your asylum is full.
What made your cop kill my trade union worker?
I've got to know, friend, I've got to know! (Chorus)

Why do these warships sail on my ocean?
Why do these bombs drop down from my sky?
Why doesn't your ship bring some food and some clothing?
I've got to know, friend, I've got to know why. (Chorus)

WOODY GUTHRIE

PAIN

THE HEROES

I dreamed of war-heroes, of wounded war-heroes
With just enough of their charms shot away
To make them more handsome. The women moved nearer
To touch their brave wounds and their hair streaked with gray.

I saw them in long ranks ascending the gang-planks;
The girls with the doughnuts were cheerful and gay.
They minded their manners and muttered their thanks;
The Chaplain advised them to watch and to pray.

They shipped these rapscallions, these sea-sick battalions
To a patriotic and picturesque spot;
They gave them new bibles and marksmen's medallions,
Compasses, maps, and committed the lot.

A fine dust has settled on all that scrap metal.
The heroes were packaged and sent home in parts
To pluck at a poppy and sew on a petal
And count the long night by the strike of their hearts.

LOUIS SIMPSON

SURGICAL WARD

They are and suffer; that is all they do;
A bandage hides the place where each is living,
His knowledge of the world restricted to
The treatment that the instruments are giving.

And lie apart like epochs from each other
—Truth in their sense is how much they can bear;
It is not talk like ours, but groans they smother—
And are remote as plants; we stand elsewhere.

For who when healthy can become a foot?
Even a scratch we can't recall when cured,
But are boist'rous in a moment and believe

In the common world of the uninjured, and cannot
Imagine isolation. Only happiness is shared,
And anger, and the idea of love.

W . H . A U D E N

HUNCHBACK GIRL:
SHE THINKS OF HEAVEN

My Father, it is surely a blue place
And straight. Right. Regular. Where I shall find
No need for scholarly nonchalance or looks
A little to the left or guards upon the
Heart to halt love that runs without crookedness
Along its crooked corridors. My Father,
It is a planned place surely. Out of coils,
Unscrewed, released, no more to be marvelous,
I shall walk straightly through most proper halls
Proper myself, princess of properness.

GWENDOLYN BROOKS

DARK GIRL

Easy on your drums,
Easy wind and rain,
And softer on your horns,
She will not dance again.

Come easy little leaves
Without a ghost of sound
From the China trees
To the fallow ground.

Easy, easy drums
And sweet leaves overhead,
Easy wind and rain;
Your dancing girl is dead.

ARNA BONTEMPS

IT'S HERE IN THE

Here in the newspaper—the wreck of the East Bound.
A photograph bound to bring on cardiac asthenia.
There is a blur that mists the page!
On one side is a gloom of dreadful harsh.
Then breaks flash lights up sheer.
There is much huge about. I suppose then
        those no's are people
    between that suffering of—
    (what more have we? for Christ's sake, no!)
Something of a full stop of it
crash of blood and the still shock
    of stark sticks and an immense swift gloss,
And two dead no's lie aghast still.
One casts a crazed eye and the other's
Closed dull.
    the heap up twists
        such
as to harden the unhard and unhard
the hardened.

RUSSELL ATKINS

HURT HAWKS

The broken pillar of the wing jags from the clotted shoulder,
The wing trails like a banner in defeat,
No more to use the sky forever but live with famine
And pain a few days: cat nor coyote
Will shorten the week of waiting for death, there is
    game without talons.
He stands under the oak-bush and waits
The lame feet of salvation; at night he remembers
    freedom
And flies in a dream, the dawns ruin it.

He is strong and pain is worse to the strong, in-
    capacity is worse.
The curs of the day come and torment him
At distance, no one but death the redeemer will
    humble that head,
The intrepid readiness, the terrible eyes.
The wild God of the world is sometimes merciful to
    those
That ask mercy, not often to the arrogant.
You do not know him, you communal people, or you
    have forgotten him;
Intemperate and savage, the hawk remembers him;
Beautiful and wild, the hawks, and men that are
    dying, remember him.

II

I'd sooner, except the penalties, kill a man than a
    hawk; but the great redtail
Had nothing left but unable misery
From the bone too shattered for mending, the wing
    that trailed under his talons when he moved.
We had fed him six weeks, I gave him freedom,
He wandered over the foreland hill and returned in
    the evening, asking for death,
Not like a beggar, still eyed with the old
Implacable arrogance. I gave him the lead gift in the
    twilight. What fell was relaxed,
Owl-downy, soft feminine feathers; but what
Soared: the fierce rush: the night-herons by the
    flooded river cried fear at its rising
Before it was quite unsheathed from reality.

ROBINSON JEFFERS

RECOLLECTIONS

SONNET TO MY MOTHER

Most near, most dear, most loved and most far,
Under the window where I often found her
Sitting as huge as Asia, seismic with laughter,
Gin and chicken helpless in her Irish hand,
Irresistible as Rabelais but most tender for
The lame dogs and hurt birds that surround her,—
She is a procession no one can follow after
But be like a little dog following a brass band.

She will not glance up at the bomber or condescend
To drop her gin and scuttle to a cellar,
But lean on the mahogany table like a mountain
Whom only faith can move, and so I send
O all my faith and all my love to tell her
That she will move from mourning into morning.

GEORGE BARKER

NUMBER 7

Fortune
        has its cookies to give out
which is a good thing

        since it's been a long time since

    that summer in Brooklyn
  when they closed off the street
      one hot day
      and the

        FIREMEN

            turned on their hoses

and all the kids ran out in it

    in the middle of the street

and there were

      maybe a couple dozen of us

           out there
with the water squirting up
      to the

      sky

      and all over

        us

there was maybe only six of us
                        kids altogether
            running around in our
                        barefeet and birthday
        suits
            and I remember Molly but then
    the firemen stopped squirting their hoses
            all of a sudden and went
                    back in
                their firehouse
                    and
        started playing pinochle again
            just as if nothing
                had ever
                    happened
while I remember Molly
                looked at me and

        ran in

because I guess really we were the only ones there

                    L A W R E N C E   F E R L I N G H E T T I

AUNT HELEN

Miss Helen Slingsby was my maiden aunt,
And lived in a small house near a fashionable square
Cared for by servants to the number of four.
Now when she died there was silence in heaven
And silence at her end of the street.
The shutters were drawn and the undertaker wiped his feet—
He was aware that this sort of thing had occurred before.
The dogs were handsomely provided for,
But shortly afterwards the parrot died too.
The Dresden clock continued ticking on the mantelpiece,
And the footman sat upon the dining-table
Holding the second housemaid on his knees—
Who had always been so careful while her mistress lived.

T. S. ELIOT

BELLS FOR JOHN WHITESIDE'S DAUGHTER

There was such speed in her little body,
And such lightness in her footfall,
It is no wonder her brown study
Astonishes us all.

Her wars were bruited in our high window.
We looked among orchard trees and beyond,
Where she took arms against her shadow,
Or harried unto the pond

The lazy geese, like a snow cloud
Dripping their snow on the green grass,
Tricking and stopping, sleepy and proud,
Who cried in goose, Alas,

For the tireless heart within the little
Lady with rod that made them rise
From their noon apple-dreams and scuttle
Goose-fashion under the skies!

But now go the bells, and we are ready,
In one house we are sternly stopped
To say we are vexed at her brown study,
Lying so primly propped.

JOHN CROWE RANSOM

ELEGY FOR JANE
(My student, thrown by a horse)

I remember the neckcurls, limp and damp as tendrils;
And her quick look, a sidelong pickerel smile;
And how, once startled into talk, the light syllables leaped for her,
And she balanced in the delight of her thought,
A wren, happy, tail into the wind,
Her song trembling the twigs and small branches.
The shade sang with her;
The leaves, their whispers turned to kissing;
And the mold sang in the bleached valleys under the rose.

Oh, when she was sad, she cast herself down into such a pure depth,
Even a father could not find her:
Scraping her cheek against straw;
Stirring the clearest water.

My sparrow, you are not here,
Waiting like a fern, making a spiny shadow.
The sides of wet stones cannot console me,
Nor the moss, wound with the last light.

If only I could nudge you from this sleep,
My maimed darling, my skittery pigeon.
Over this damp grave I speak the words of my love:
I, with no rights in this matter,
Neither father nor lover.

THEODORE ROETHKE

THE ELEMENTARY SCENE

Looking back in my mind I can see
The white sun like a tin plate
Over the wooden turning of the weeds;
The street jerking—a wet swing—
To end by the wall the children sang.

The thin grass by the girls' door,
Trodden on, straggling, yellow and rotten,
And the gaunt field with its one tied cow—
The dead land waking sadly to my life—
Stir, and curl deeper in the eyes of time.

The rotting pumpkin under the stairs
Bundled with switches and the cold ashes
Still holds for me, in its unwavering eyes,
The stinking shapes of cranes and witches,
Their path slanting down the pumpkin's sky.

Its stars beckon through the frost like cottages
(Homes of the Bear, the Hunter—of that absent star,
The dark where the flushed child struggles into sleep)
Till, leaning a lifetime to the comforter,
I float above the small limbs like their dream:

I, I, the future that mends everything.

RANDALL JARRELL

FERN HILL

Now as I was young and easy under the apple boughs
About the lilting house and happy as the grass was green,
        The night above the dingle starry,
            Time let me hail and climb
        Golden in the heydays of his eyes,
And honored among wagons I was prince of the apple towns
And once below a time I lordly had the trees and leaves
            Trail with daisies and barley
        Down the rivers of the windfall light.

And as I was green and carefree, famous among the barns
About the happy yard and singing as the farm was home,
        In the sun that is young once only,
            Time let me play and be
        Golden in the mercy of his means,
And green and golden I was huntsman and herdsman, the calves
Sang to my horn, the foxes on the hills barked clear and cold,
            And the sabbath rang slowly
In the pebbles of the holy streams.

All the sun long it was running, it was lovely, the hay
Fields high as the house, the tunes from the chimneys, it was air
        And playing, lovely and watery
            And fire green as grass.
        And nightly under the simple stars
As I rode to sleep the owls were bearing the farm away,
All the moon long I heard, blessed among stables, the night-jars
        Flying with the ricks, and the horses
            Flashing into the dark.

And then to awake, and the farm, like a wanderer white
With the dew, come back, the cock on his shoulder: it was all
     Shining, it was Adam and maiden,
        The sky gathered again
      And the sun grew round that very day.
So it must have been after the birth of the simple light
In the first, spinning place, the spellbound horses walking warm
     Out of the whinnying green stable
       On to the fields of praise.

And honored among foxes and pheasants by the gay house
Under the new made clouds and happy as the heart was long,
     In the sun born over and over,
       I ran my heedless ways,
     My wishes raced through the house high hay
And nothing I cared, at my sky blue trades, that time allows
In all his tuneful turning so few and such morning songs
     Before the children green and golden
       Follow him out of grace,
Nothing I cared, in the lamb white days, that time would take me
Up to the swallow thronged loft by the shadow of my hand,
     In the moon that is always rising,
       Nor that riding to sleep
     I should hear him fly with the high fields
And wake to the farm forever fled from the childless land.
Oh as I was young and easy in the mercy of his means,
      Time held me green and dying
     Though I sang in my chains like the sea.

DYLAN THOMAS

INDEX OF FIRST LINES

INDEX OF AUTHORS AND TITLES

ACKNOWLEDGMENTS

"Little Brand New Baby (For Andrew Arthur Okun, Born September 29, 1962)," words and music by Tom Paxton: © copyright 1962, 1965 by Cherry Lane Music, Inc. Used by permission. All rights reserved.

"The Name" by Robert Creeley: copyright © 1961 by Robert Creeley. Reprinted with the permission of Charles Scribner's Sons from *For Love* by Robert Creeley.

"Taught Me Purple" by Evelyn Tooley Hunt: published in *Negro Digest*, February 1964. Reprinted by permission of the author.

"Mother to Son" by Langston Hughes: copyright 1926 by Alfred A. Knopf, Inc., and renewed 1954 by Langston Hughes. Reprinted from *Selected Poems* by Langston Hughes, by permission of the publisher.

"That Dark Other Mountain" by Robert Francis: reprinted with the permission of Robert Francis and the University of Massachusetts Press from *Come Out into the Sun: Poems New and Selected*. Copyright by Robert Francis.

"What Shall He Tell That Son?" by Carl Sandburg: from *The People, Yes* by Carl Sandburg. Copyright 1936 by Harcourt, Brace & World, Inc.; renewed 1964 by Carl Sandburg. Reprinted by permission of the publishers.

"My Papa's Waltz" by Theodore Roethke: copyright 1942 by Hearst Magazine, Inc. From *The Collected Poems of Theodore Roethke*. Reprinted by permission of Doubleday & Company, Inc.

"The Empty Woman" by Gwendolyn Brooks: copyright © 1963 by Gwendolyn Brooks Blakely. From *Selected Poems* (1963) by Gwendolyn Brooks. Reprinted by permission of Harper & Row, Publishers.

"Stark Boughs on the Family Tree" by Mary Oliver: © 1968 by The New York Times Company and reprinted by permission. Copyright © 1968 by Mary Oliver and used by permission.

"Home Burial" by Robert Frost: from *Complete Poems of Robert Frost*. Copyright 1930, 1939 by Holt, Rinehart and Winston, Inc. Copyright © 1958 by Robert Frost. Copyright © 1967 by Lesley Frost Ballantine. Reprinted by permission of Holt, Rinehart and Winston, Inc.

"Declaration of Independence" by Wolcott Gibbs: copyright 1948 by G. Schirmer, Inc. Used by permission.

"Drawing by Ronnie C., Grade One" by Ruth Lechlitner: copyright 1967 by Saturday Review, Inc. Reprinted by permission of the author. First published in *Saturday Review*.

"My Parents Kept Me from Children Who Were Rough" by Stephen Spender: copyright 1934 and renewed 1962 by Stephen Spender. Reprinted from *Collected Poems*

1928–1953 by Stephen Spender, by permission of Random House, Inc., and Faber and Faber, Ltd.

"Boy at the Window" by Richard Wilbur: copyright 1952 by The New Yorker Magazine, Inc. Reprinted from *Things of This World* by Richard Wilbur, by permission of Harcourt, Brace & World, Inc. First published in *The New Yorker*.

"The Ballad of the Light-Eyed Girl" by Gwendolyn Brooks: copyright 1949 by Gwendolyn Brooks Blakely. From *Selected Poems* (1963) by Gwendolyn Brooks. Reprinted by permission of Harper & Row, Publishers.

"The Ballad of Chocolate Mabbie" by Gwendolyn Brooks: copyright 1945 by Gwendolyn Brooks Blakely. From *Selected Poems* (1963) by Gwendolyn Brooks. Reprinted by permission of Harper & Row, Publishers.

"Janet Waking" by John Crowe Ransom: copyright 1927 by Alfred A. Knopf, Inc., and renewed 1952 by John Crowe Ransom. Reprinted from *Selected Poems*, Revised Edition, by John Crowe Ransom, by permission of the publisher.

"Prayer Before Birth" by Louis MacNeice: from *The Collected Poems of Louis MacNeice*, edited by E. R. Dodds. Copyright © 1966. The Estate of Louis MacNeice. Reprinted by permission of Oxford University Press, Inc., and Faber and Faber, Ltd.

"Portrait of a Girl with Comic Book" by Phyllis McGinley: from *Times Three* by Phyllis McGinley. Copyright 1952 by Phyllis McGinley. First published in *The New Yorker*. Reprinted by permission of The Viking Press, Inc.

"Fifteen" by William Stafford: from *The Rescued Year* by William Stafford. Copyright © 1964 by William E. Stafford. By permission of Harper & Row, Publishers.

"The Dreamer" by William Childress: copyright © 1966 by Harper's Magazine, Inc. Reprinted from the March 1966 issue of *Harper's Magazine* by permission of the author.

"The Cave" by Glenn W. Dresbach: from Glen W. Dresbach's *Collected Poems*. The Caxton Printers, Ltd., Caldwell, Idaho.

"Preface to a Twenty Volume Suicide Note" by LeRoi Jones: copyright © 1961 by LeRoi Jones, Corinth Books, New York.

"Pastoral" by William Carlos Williams: from *Collected Earlier Poems* by William Carlos Williams. Copyright 1938 by William Carlos Williams. Reprinted by permission of New Directions Publishing Corporation.

"Kennedy" by Molly Kazan: reprinted by permission of Stein and Day, Incorporated. Copyright © 1963 by Elia Kazan.

"Yet Do I Marvel" by Countee Cullen: copyright 1925 by Harper & Brothers; renewed 1953 by Ida M. Cullen. From *On These I Stand* (1947) by Countee Cullen. Reprinted by permission of Harper & Row, Publishers.

"The Negro Speaks of Rivers" by Langston Hughes: copyright 1926 by Alfred A. Knopf, Inc., and renewed 1954 by Langston Hughes. Reprinted from *Selected Poems* by Langston Hughes, by permission of the publisher.

"Powwow" by W. D. Snodgrass: Copyright © 1963 by W. D. Snodgrass. From *After Experience* (1968) by W. D. Snodgrass. Originally appeared in *The New Yorker* and reprinted by permission of Harper & Row, Publishers, Incorporated.

"Florida Road Workers" by Langston Hughes: from *The Panther and the Lash* by Langston Hughes. © copyright 1967 by Arna Bontemps and George Houston Bass. Reprinted by permission of Alfred A. Knopf, Inc.

"Pastures of Plenty," words and music by Woody Guthrie: TRO ⓒ copyright 1960 and 1963 by Ludlow Music, Inc., New York, N.Y. Used by permission.

"Caliban in the Coal Mines" by Louis Untermeyer: copyright 1914 by Harcourt, Brace & World, Inc.; renewed 1942 by Louis Untermeyer. Reprinted from his volume *Long Feud* by permission of the publishers.

"Sunday Afternoon" by Denise Levertov: from *The Jacob's Ladder* by Denise Levertov. Copyright ⓒ 1958 by Denise Levertov Goodman. Reprinted by permission of New Directions Publishing Corporation.

"Two Voices in a Meadow" by Richard Wilbur: ⓒ 1957 by Richard Wilbur. Reprinted from his volume *Advice to a Prophet and Other Poems* by permission of Harcourt, Brace & World, Inc. First published in *The New Yorker*.

"Gone Away" by Denise Levertov: from *O Taste and See* by Denise Levertov Goodman. Copyright ⓒ 1964 by Denise Levertov Goodman. Reprinted by permission of New Directions Publishing Corporation.

"The Rebel" by Mari E. Evans: first published in *American Negro Poetry*. Used by permission of the author.

"Bendix" by John Updike: ⓒ 1959 by John Updike. Reprinted from *Telephone Poles and Other Poems* by John Updike, by permission of Alfred A. Knopf, Inc. First published in *The New Yorker*.

"At Breakfast" by May Swenson: copyright 1955 by May Swenson. First published in *The New Yorker*. Reprinted with the permission of Charles Scribner's Sons from *To Mix with Time* by May Swenson.

"Sonic Boom" by John Updike: ⓒ 1959 by John Updike. Reprinted from *Telephone Poles and Other Poems* by John Updike, by permission of Alfred A. Knopf, Inc.

"Ice Cream" by Jonathan Price: Copyright ⓒ 1970 by Jonathan Price. First published in the *Yale Alumni Magazine*, December, 1968.

"The Bat" by Theodore Roethke: copyright 1938 by Theodore Roethke. From the book *The Collected Poems of Theodore Roethke*. Reprinted by permission of Doubleday & Company, Inc.

"For a Lamb" by Richard Eberhart: from *Collected Poems 1930–1960* by Richard Eberhart. ⓒ 1960 by Richard Eberhart. Reprinted by permission of Oxford University Press, Inc., and Chatto and Windus, Ltd.

"Summer: West Side" by John Updike: ⓒ 1960 by John Updike. Reprinted from *Telephone Poles and Other Poems* by John Updike, by permission of Alfred A. Knopf, Inc. First published in *The New Yorker*.

"Auto Wreck" by Karl Shapiro: copyright 1941 by Karl Shapiro. Reprinted from *Poems 1940–1953* by Karl Shapiro, by permission of Random House, Inc.

"The Yachts" by William Carlos Williams: from *Collected Earlier Poems* by William Carlos Williams. Copyright 1938 by William Carlos Williams. Reprinted by permission of New Directions Publishing Corporation.

"Crystal Moment" by Robert P. Tristram Coffin: reprinted with the permission of The Macmillan Company from *Collected Poems of Robert P. Tristram Coffin*. Copyright 1932 by The Macmillan Company; renewed 1960 by Margaret Halvasa.

"Traveling Through the Dark" by William Stafford: copyright ⓒ 1960 by William Stafford. From *Traveling Through the Dark* (1962) by William Stafford. Reprinted by permission of Harper & Row, Publishers.

From "The Man with the Blue Guitar" by Wallace Stevens: Copyright 1936 and renewed 1964 by Elsie Stevens and Holly Stevens. Reprinted from *The Collected Poems of Wallace Stevens* by permission of Alfred A. Knopf, Inc.

"Number 20" by Lawrence Ferlinghetti: from *A Coney Island of The Mind* by Lawrence Ferlinghetti. Copyright © 1955, 1958 by Lawrence Ferlinghetti. Reprinted by permission of New Directions Publishing Corporation.

"Lucy in the Sky with Diamonds" by The Beatles: from *The Beatles Illustrated Lyrics,* edited by Alan Aldridge. Lyrics copyright © 1962, 1963, 1964, 1965, 1966, 1967, 1968, 1969 by Northern Songs Limited (London). Illustrations and text copyright © 1969 by Alan Aldridge Associates Limited (London). A Seymour Lawrence Book/Delacorte Press. Used by permission.

"Museum" by Louis MacNeice: from *The Collected Poems of Louis MacNeice,* edited by E. R. Dodds. Copyright © 1966 The Estate of Louis MacNeice. Reprinted by permission of Oxford University Press, Inc., and reprinted by Faber and Faber, Ltd.

"Suburban Madrigal" by John Updike: © copyright 1959 by John Updike. Reprinted from *Telephone Poles and Other Poems* by John Updike, by permission of Alfred A. Knopf, Inc. First published in *The New Yorker*.

"Sand Hill Road" by Morton Grosser: reprinted by permission of Curtis Brown, Ltd. Copyright © 1966 by Harper's Magazine, Inc. Reprinted from the April 1966 issue of *Harper's Magazine*.

"The Lifeguard" by James Dickey: copyright © 1961 by James Dickey. Reprinted from *Drowning with Others* by James Dickey, by permission of Wesleyan University Press. First published in *The New Yorker*.

"Sketch from Loss of Memory" by Sonya Dorman: copyright 1968 by Saturday Review, Inc. Reprinted by permission of the author and *Saturday Review*.

"She's Leaving Home" by The Beatles: from *The Beatles Illustrated Lyrics,* edited by Alan Aldridge. Lyrics copyright © 1962, 1963, 1964, 1965, 1966, 1967, 1968, 1969 by Northern Songs Limited (London). Illustrations and text copyright © 1969 by Alan Aldridge Associates Limted (London). A Seymour Lawrence Book/Delacorte Press. Used by permission.

"Southbound on the Freeway" by May Swenson: copyright © 1963 by May Swenson. First published in *The New Yorker*. Reprinted with the permission of Charles Scribner's Sons from *To Mix with Time* by May Swenson.

"Little Boxes," words and music by Malvina Reynolds: © copyright 1962 by Schroder Music Company (ASCAP).

"Target" by R. P. Lister: reprinted by permission of International Famous Agency, Inc. © 1959 The New Yorker Magazine, Inc.

"next to of course god america i" by e. e. cummings: copyright 1926 by Horace Liveright; renewed 1954 by E. E. Cummings. Reprinted from his volume *Poems 1923–1954* by permission of Harcourt, Brace & World, Inc.

"Vapor Trail Reflected in the Frog Pond" by Galway Kinnell: from *Body Rags* by Galway Kinnell. Copyright © 1965, 1966, 1967 by Galway Kinnell. Reprinted by permission of the Publisher, Houghton Mifflin Company.

"The Body Politic" by Donald Hall: reprinted by permission of Curtis Brown, Ltd. Copyright © 1955 by Donald Hall.

"The Unknown Citizen" by W. H. Auden: copyright 1940 and renewed 1968 by W. H. Auden. Reprinted from *Collected Shorter Poems 1927–1957* by W. H. Auden, by permission of Random House, Inc.

"pity this busy monster,manunkind" by e. e. cummings: copyright 1944 by E. E. Cummings. Reprinted from his volume *Poems 1923–1954* by permission of Harcourt, Brace & World, Inc.

"The Angry Man" by Phyllis McGinley: from *Times Three* by Phyllis McGinley. Copyright 1954 by Phyllis McGinley. Reprinted by permission of The Viking Press, Inc.

"Thoughts While Driving Home" by John Updike: © copyright 1959 by John Updike. Reprinted from *Telephone Poles and Other Poems* by permission of Alfred A. Knopf, Inc.

"Confession Overheard in a Subway" by Kenneth Fearing: from *New and Selected Poems* by Kenneth Fearing. Copyright © 1965 by Kenneth Fearing. Reprinted by permission of Indiana University Press.

"Loneliness" by Brooks Jenkins: reprinted by permission of Scholastic Magazines, Inc. Copyright 1935 by Scholastic Magazines, Inc.

"A Ritual to Read to Each Other" by William Stafford: copyright William Stafford and used by permission of the author. First published in *The Hudson Review*, Vol. VII, No. 3.

"How She Resolved to Act" by Merrill Moore: copyright Ann Leslie Moore and used by permission.

"For Anne" and "Song" by Leonard Cohen: from *Selected Poems 1956–1968* by Leonard Cohen. All rights reserved. Reprinted by permission of The Viking Press, Inc., and the Canadian Publishers, McClelland and Stewart Limited, Toronto.

"To Be in Love" by Gwendolyn Brooks: copyright © 1963 by Gwendolyn Brooks Blakely. From *Selected Poems* (1963) by Gwendolyn Brooks. Reprinted by permission of Harper & Row, Publishers.

"Places, Loved Ones" by Philip Larkin: reprinted from *The Less Deceived* by permission of The Marvell Press, Hessle, Yorkshire, England.

"somewhere i have never travelled" by e. e. cummings: copyright 1931, 1959 by E. E. Cummings. Reprinted from his volume *Poems 1923–1954* by permission of Harcourt, Brace & World, Inc.

"For Hettie" by LeRoi Jones: copyright © 1961 by LeRoi Jones. Published by Corinth Books.

"The River-Merchant's Wife: A Letter" by Rihaku: from *Personae* by Ezra Pound. Copyright 1926 by Ezra Pound. Reprinted by permission of New Directions Publishing Corporation.

"The Sonnet-Ballad" by Gwendolyn Brooks: copyright 1949 by Gwendolyn Brooks Blakely. From *Selected Poems* (1963) by Gwendolyn Brooks. Reprinted by permission of Harper & Row, Publishers.

"Where Have All the Flowers Gone?" by Pete Seeger: copyright © 1961 by Fall River Music, Inc. All rights reserved. Used by permission.

"Naming of Parts" by Henry Reed: from *A Map of Verona and Other Poems*, copyright 1947 by Henry Reed. Reprinted by permission of Harcourt, Brace & World, Inc., and Jonathan Cape, Ltd.

"Of Bombs and Boys" by Richard Corbin: reprinted by permission of the author.

"my sweet old etcetera" by e. e. cummings: copyright 1926 by Horace Liveright; renewed 1954 by E. E. Cummings. Reprinted from *Poems 1923–1954* by permission of Harcourt, Brace & World, Inc.

"The Death of the Ball Turret Gunner" by Randall Jarrell: reprinted with the permission of Farrar, Straus & Giroux, Inc., from *Complete Poems* by Randall Jarrell. Copyright 1945 by Mrs. Randall Jarrell.

"An Irish Airman Foresees His Death" by W. B. Yeats: reprinted with the permission of The Macmillan Company from *Collected Poems of William Butler Yeats*. Copyright 1919 by The Macmillan Company; renewed 1947 by Bertha Georgie Yeats.

"Ultima Ratio Regum" by Stephen Spender: copyright 1942 by Stephen Spender. Reprinted from *Collected Poems 1928–1953* by Stephen Spender, by permission of Random House, Inc., and Faber and Faber, Ltd.

"The Conscientious Objector" by Karl Shapiro: copyright 1947 by Karl Shapiro. Reprinted from *Selected Poems* by Karl Shapiro, by permission of Random House, Inc.

"I've Got to Know" by Woody Guthrie: © copyright 1950 by Stormking Music, Inc. All rights reserved. Used by permission.

"The Heroes" by Louis Simpson: reprinted with the permission of Charles Scribner's Sons from *Good News of Death and Other Poems* by Louis Simpson. Copyright 1955 by Louis Simpson (*Poems of Today II*).

"Surgical Ward" by W. H. Auden: copyright 1945 by W. H. Auden. Reprinted from *Collected Shorter Poems 1927–1957* by W. H. Auden, by permission of Random House, Inc.

"Hunchback Girl: She Thinks of Heaven" by Gwendolyn Brooks: copyright 1945 by Gwendolyn Brooks Blakely. From *Selected Poems* (1963) by Gwendolyn Brooks. Reprinted by permission of Harper & Row, Publishers.

"Dark Girl" by Arna Bontemps: reprinted by permission of Harold Ober Associates Incorporated. Copyright © 1941 by Arna Bontemps.

"It's Here In The" by Russell Atkins: copyright 1952 by *Beloit Poetry Journal*. Published in *American Negro Poetry*. Used by permission of the author.

"Hurt Hawks" by Robinson Jeffers: copyright 1928 and renewed 1956 by Robinson Jeffers. Reprinted from *The Selected Poetry of Robinson Jeffers* by permission of Random House, Inc.

"Sonnet to My Mother" by George Barker: from *Collected Poems 1930–1965*. Copyright © 1957, 1962, and 1965 by George Granville Barker. Reprinted by permission of October House, Inc.

"Number 7" by Lawrence Ferlinghetti: from *A Coney Island of the Mind* by Lawrence Ferlinghetti. Copyright © 1955, 1958 by Lawrence Ferlinghetti. Reprinted by permission of New Directions Publishing Corporation.

"Aunt Helen" by T. S. Eliot: from *Collected Poems 1909–1962* by T. S. Eliot. Copyright 1936 by Harcourt, Brace & World, Inc. Copyright © 1963, 1964 by T. S. Eliot. Reprinted by permission of the publishers.

"Bells for John Whiteside's Daughter" by John Crowe Ransom: copyright 1924 by Alfred A. Knopf, Inc., and renewed 1955 by John Crowe Ransom. Reprinted from *Selected Poems*, Revised Edition, by John Crowe Ransom, by permission of the publisher.

"Elegy for Jane" by Theodore Roethke: copyright 1950 by Theodore Roethke. From *The Collected Poems of Theodore Roethke*. Reprinted by permission of Doubleday & Company, Inc.

"The Elementary Scene" by Randall Jarrell: from *The Woman at the Washington Zoo* by Randall Jarrell, published by Atheneum. Copyright © 1960 by Randall Jarrell. Reprinted by permission of Atheneum.

"Fern Hill" by Dylan Thomas: from *Collected Poems* by Dylan Thomas. Copyright 1946 by New Directions Publishing Corporation. Reprinted by permission of New Directions Publishing Corporation.